Flowering Trees

FOR CENTRAL AND SOUTH FLORIDA GARDENS

Genesis 2-9: "And out of the ground made the Lord God every tree that is pleasant to the sight and good for food."

Flowering Trees

FOR CENTRAL AND SOUTH FLORIDA GARDENS

Maxine Fortune Schuetz

GREAT *OUTDOORS* PUBLISHING CO.
4747 -28th STREET NORTH
ST. PETERSBURG, FLORIDA 33708

123618

ISBN: 8200-0410-3

Printed in the United States of America

This book is dedicated
to the memory of the late Charlie Allyn.
His life-long love of flowering trees
is still evident in the colorful blossoms
that beautify the grounds of the Great Outdoors.

Table of Contents

About the Author

Maxine Fortune Schuetz began life far from Florida, in Seattle, Washington, where she studied botany. She has ever since managed to combine her knowledge and love of plants with her considerable artistic talent and skill. She worked for a number of years as a landscape designer for several nurseries in the Fort Lauderdale, Pompano Beach area; her perspective renderings of homes, churches and other buildings are quite well known, not only here but in many parts of the country.

Sketching trees and plants came naturally to her wherever she found herself — as an ardent worker in the Countryside Garden Club of Augusta, or working for various nurseries in Augusta, Georgia and Hilton Head, South Carolina (Hillside Nursery, The Greenery).

Many of the trees in this book were sketched twenty-five or thirty years ago. She credits the late Art vonWaldburg with much of the material used in describing tropical trees. Son of a well known landscape architect in the New York area, Art vonWaldburg was an outstanding landscape architect with over thirty-five years experience in South Florida. He spent eight years with Dade County Parks Department.

While living in Florida, Maxine painted murals with Leone Nicholls for several years and continues her painting in Georgia with murals in homes and business establishments, as well as pictures of historical churches, homes and landscape scenes.

Each of the illustrations in this book were painted "from life" — from a tree representative of the species. Some grew in private yards, but most were sketched in Florida nurseries.

After having been a widow for eleven years, Maxine, in 1977, married Raymond (Tex) Schuetz of Texas. They reside on a beautiful lake near Lincolnton, Georgia.

Introduction

Some of the flowering trees in this book may be unfamiliar to many Florida residents, but each is beautiful, or useful, or interesting; many of them deserve to become more common in our Florida landscape.

We know now that the world's green garment of trees is vital to the very existence of life as we know it on our planet earth. Aside from the grand scheme, trees can improve our daily lives, even from an economic standpoint. A shaded house requires far fewer dollars for air conditioning than does one bombarded by day long sun (especially tropical sun). And if that were not true, we would still want trees for their aesthetic value. To live with trees is to live with beauty. In Florida we have so many varieties that we could consider them an artist's palette from which to paint our landscapes, as colorful as any painter could wish.

Planeloads of people land in Holland every year just to view the vast fields of tulips; our own Washington, D.C. is ethereally transformed each spring by the hundreds of cherry trees that line its thoroughfares. To engage in a bit of fantasy, imagine a flower garden, miles across, planted with thirty foot tall Queen Elizabeth rose bushes. No, of course rose bushes won't grow thirty feet tall! But Jacaranda and Peltophorum, and Bombax trees will. To continue our fantasy, now imagine a Florida city in which, when its streets were first laid out, every street, avenue, lawn and parking lot, had been lined with a particular flowering tree. Fields of tulips couldn't hold a candle to such an immense concentration of color; planeloads of people would also, no doubt make pilgrimages to such a Flower Garden City. We admit to the impracticality of such a plan and confess we are simply playing a game of fantasy with such an idea. However, to the pleasure of all who see it, a "giant flower garden" is just what we achieve when we plant flowering trees.

There is variety in form and character as well as color in our trees. Some lend themselves to umbrella service — large, deciduous, shading the house in summer and losing leaves for a brief time in winter when the sunshine may be welcome. Some lend themselves to espaliering against a wall, training around an arbor, or creating a wall for privacy or safety. Some are weeping forms that lend a vertical "waterfall effect" to the scene. Some grow into picturesque shapes that frame and enhance an interesting view of the sea or lake. There is as much room to be creative in gardening as there is in painting a picture. In a way, it *is* "painting a picture".

There is a right tree for every spot. The one that frames your seascape must be tolerant of salt, and if you're concerned about our dwindling water supply, or are planning a xeriscaped garden, choose one that is not excessively thirsty. (Fortunately, many of our flowering trees do withstand drought quite well, once they are established.) We have included such characteristics in the brief descriptions of this book, to help you in doing what would be most gratifying to the author of this book. Plant a tree!

THE PUBLISHER

African Tulip Tree

African Tulip Tree
Flame of the Forest
Fountain Tree

Spathodea Campanulata

This stately evergreen tree, often growing fifty feet high, is a native of tropical Africa. It was discovered there in 1787 by Palisot Beauvois. However, it is now found growing throughout the tropics of the western hemisphere. The unopened flower buds retain water, and when squeezed act like a water pistol; this gives rise to yet another common name – Fountain Tree.

The bark is light gray and the wood soft and brittle, making it subject to damage by high winds. A most resilient tree, though, it is not killed by being broken off or even frozen to the ground, and will come back from the roots.

The leaves are pinnate, made up of nine to nineteen large, ovate, dark green leaflets, each up to four inches long. The leaflets are leathery with prominent veins.

Both growth habit and blooming periods are irregular. The clusters of bright red flowers may be borne on branch ends throughout the year. The individual, four-inch, scarlet blooms are cup shaped, with five frilled irregular lobes edged in bright yellow. Growing in a circular mass, the center is formed of densely compact buds. Only a few buds on the outside of the circle open at a time, thus maintaining a long blooming period. Following the bloom, the winged seeds develop in unusual boat-shaped, two-foot long pods.

A rapid grower in fertile, well-drained soil, the African Tulip tree will thrive under most conditions. It doesn't like the beach, as it has no salt tolerance, but otherwise needs only a frost free area in full sun to grow and flourish. Also, once established, it is fairly drought-resistant, making it a good choice for our water-starved areas.

Use it in landscaping as a parkway tree or a colorful shade tree in the garden.

There is a yellow form, rare in Florida but grown extensively in Hawaii.

8

see color page 50

9

Angel's Trumpet

Angel's Trumpet
Datura

Datura arborea
Datura brugmansia

This very conspicuous, bushy, small evergreen tree is native in the Peruvian Andes. It grows to only fifteen feet, with bright colored bark and very brittle wood. *Datura* is an old Arabic name.

The thick leaves, ten inches long, ovate, lanceolate, and grayish green, are soft and shiny.

Blooming continually, the trumpet shaped, drooping flowers hang like ornaments on a Christmas tree. They are about ten inches long, white with greenish veins, having fine, thin segments, each coming to a twisted point. The calyx is spathe-like, enwraps the end of the top of the tube, is split and slightly pointed. In the evening they give off an exotic musk scent. Both the flowers and the leaves are highly poisonous if eaten, but smoking the leaves was once a folk remedy for asthma — probably at considerable risk. The capsular fruit, to two and a half inches long, is also poisonous.

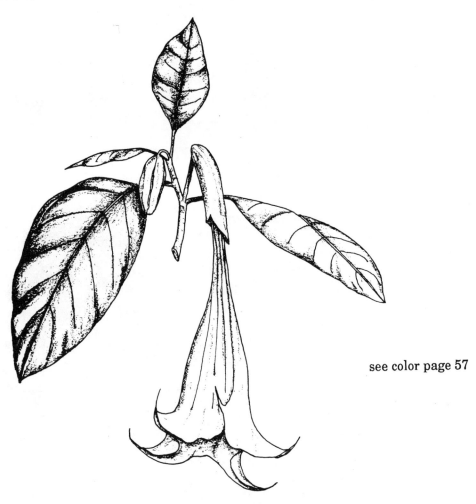

see color page 57

The *Datura* grows rapidly in sandy loam soil. It is tolerant of neither salt nor drought. Required are full sun and a frost free climate. It is propagated by seeds or cuttings.

Away from the beach, and away from small children who might find its "trumpets" alluring, the Angel's Trumpet is a spectacular addition as a specimen tree in the garden.

There are numerous varieties. Among them is a peach colored variety, *D. suaveolens arborea* that is native in Brazil. The leaves and the flowers grow up to a foot long. *D. stomonium* is the North American Jimson Weed, which is also poisonous. It grows to three to five feet and has white or violet four inch flowers. All are distant relatives of our non-poisonous potatoes and tomatoes.

Beauty Leaf

Beauty Leaf
Mast Wood
Kamani

Calophyllum inophyllum

Many of our flowering trees are limited to inland locations, as salt spray would quickly destroy them. Not so for this one. Indigenous to the shores of the Indian and west Pacific Oceans, it thrives on sandy beach conditions. However, it is not limited to that environment; it also does well in inland gardens. In its native land it grows to sixty feet, but in Florida it usually reaches only half that height.

Its common name, Beauty Leaf, is an apt description. The large leaves form a dense, dark green crown, with foliage often near the ground. The evergreen leaves are opposite, shiny dark green, oblong and leathery, up to six inches long and three inches wide. Tips are blunt, and numerous closely parallel veins extend from the prominent midrib to the margin.

Appearing in spring, the small, china-white, one inch flowers have a sweet fragrance that attracts innumerable bees and other insects. The blooms are in upright racemes, to seven inches long, with white stalks; thick yellow stamens grow from a coral pink ovary. The fruit that follows the bloom is a one to one-and-one-half inch long drupe which is toxic.

see color page 61

12

Beauty Leaf grows rapidly in sandy loam soil, preferably in full sun. Not among our most drought resistant trees, it needs a fair amount of moisture for best results. Coastal winds may distort it to irregular (and often picturesque!) shapes but it can be pruned to a more conventional form. It can withstand light frost without injury.

C. antillonum, native to the West Indies, is similar in foliage but produces less abundant bloom.

Bombax

Red Silk Cotton
Kapok Tree

Bombax ceiba
Bombax malabaricum

The tree usually called Kapok in Florida is not Kapok but a Bombax tree. It is native to India, Java and tropical America. It is the national tree of Guatemala and was considered sacred by the ancient Mexican Maya. (The true Kapok tree is *Ceiba pentandra* and is not common in Florida.)

Because the Bombax tree grows to such a mammoth size and is so spectacular when in bloom, specimens have become tourist attractions in many tropical cities. It grows too large for most home planting and is more often used in parks and municipal properties where there is ample space for its development. Deciduous and fast growing, the tree may exceed a hundred feet in height; the wide, spreading branches grow in tiers at right angles to the trunk, which is often nine feet thick. On older trees, the surface buttress roots may extend thirty feet or more. Young trees may have many sharp spines on the trunks, but old specimens appear smooth.

The grayish-green, digitately compound leaves, up to seven inches in length, grow at the end of long slender leaf stalks. These leaflets, usually five to nine in number, are connected to a single point like fingers on a hand. The tree drops its leaves before blooming.

In late February or early March, red flowers appear in profusion. The large, heavy, six-inch blooms consist of five velvety, thick petals, clustered near the branch ends. Centers of the blossoms are filled with scarlet stamens tipped with purple anthers.

Bombax flowers secrete a nectar which is very attractive to birds. The fallen blossoms form a carpet on the ground and are eaten by squirrels and other animals. In Burma, the flowers are used as a curry vegetable. Following the bloom, seed pods appear. They are oval, six inches long, and are filled with small, hard, pea-shaped, cotton-covered seeds in a wooly substance which is sometimes used for fiber in stuffing pillows, life jackets, etc. It is this silky material, much like the "kapok" of the *Ceiba pentandra* (Kapok tree) that has contributed to the confusion in the nomenclature. During World War II, some commercial use was made of the Bombax fiber when it was collected for use in life jackets for the military.

Propagation is by seeds. The Bombax tree rates poorly in salt tolerance – but if grown away from the beach, it is a rapid grower when given a tropical climate, fertile, sandy loam soil, and full sun.

14

see color front cover

15

Bottle Brush

Showy Bottle Brush   *Callistemon spp.*

There are a dozen varieties of *Callistemon* ("beautiful stamen"), native to Australia, which have adapted beautifully to widespread use in Florida gardens. Several characteristics are common to most. All have light green or grayish-green lanceolate leaves. The flowers are borne at (or near) branch ends. The tiny flowers are inconspicuous; the light, cream colored blooms are almost obscured by dense tufts of bright red to dark red stamens. Many are hardy enough for most of Florida, and all are fairly salt tolerant. All need full sun.

While *C. rigidus* grows in an upright shrubby habit, others have long, drooping branches much like a weeping willow. The bottle brushes are related to the *Melaleuca* ("punk" or "cajeput" tree) and bloom in a similar manner; the flowers are replaced by small, gray, capsular seed pods along the stem, and the branch ends continue to grow beyond the bloom stem. Blooms appear periodically throughout the summer, but most profusely in spring.

C. speciosus grows twenty to thirty feet tall and is among the showiest, with its deep red flower spikes. *C. viminalis* bears similar flowers and is most graceful, with long willowy branches. New leaf growth is covered with pinkish down. *C. rigidus* is probably more cold hardy than others, and also most tolerant of dry conditions. Among these, and several other varieties that may be offered, there is some variation in hardiness, and it may be best to consult local nurseries to determine the species best suited to your area. (Also, there is considerable confusion as to common names given to various species.)

Propagation is by seeds or cuttings of mature wood. Some people gather the seeds in summer, and store them away until the capsules open. They are then planted the following spring, preferably where they are to grow. Small specimens may be transplanted easily – large plants only with difficulty.

The Bottle Brushes are beautiful, hardy, can withstand heavy winds, and can weather drought and salt air better than many of the other flowering trees.

16

see color page 65

17

Coral Tree

Coral Tree   *Erythrina indica*

There is much confusion over which name goes with which species among the dozens of Erythrina trees that may be grown in the southern half of Florida. *Erythras* is the Greek word for red, which only inadequately describes these spectacular blossoms. Identification of the numerous species is best left to the experts.

The *E. indica* is large, spreading and deciduous. It grows to twenty-five or thirty feet with thick, angular branches that may be armed with small black prickles. (Even the leaves of some trees have tiny thorns.) The bright green compound leaves consist of three broad, egg-shaped leaflets, which fall in January and February; the tree is thus usually bare in spring when the large, rich red flowers appear in clusters at the end of the branches. Flower petals break out of the split side of a pointed calyx, with one petal longer than the others. All the flowers in the same whorl open on the same day. They have no scent. Curved, foot-long pods containing dark red, poisonous seeds appear after the bloom.

In a frost free area, with rich fertile soil and full sun, this tree is moderately fast growing and is a very showy addition to the landscape as a specimen or street tree. It is propagated by cuttings or seeds. Blossoms are pollinated by the birds which are attracted to the sweet nectar they find there. Salt tolerance is poor to fair, but this tree withstands drought well.

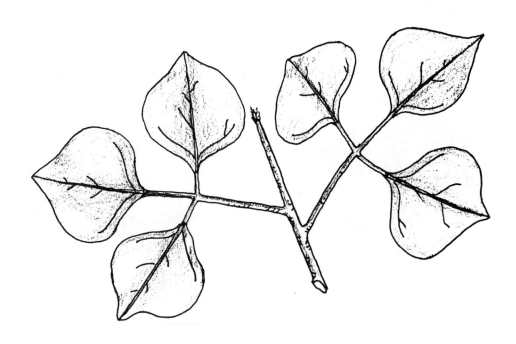

Another variety grown in Florida is *E. crista-gallii*, a native of Brazil. It is sometimes sold as "Baby Tears". It is semi-evergreen, bearing its red, pea-shaped flowers along with leaves.

E. poeppigiana is a large (to eighty feet), thorny Peruvian tree with an abundance of scarlet flowers in winter, usually when the tree is leafless. In central and South America it is used as a shade tree for cocoa bushes.

see color page 74

Dwarf Poinciana

Dwarf Poinciana
Barbados Pride

Caesalpinia pulcherrima
(syn. *Poinciana pulcherrima*)

This small evergreen tree, usually growing to around ten feet, is prickly
and straggly of habit, but is grown for the many clusters of scarlet and
yellow flowers. It is a familiar tree in southern Florida and grows wild in
Mexico, South America and other tropical countries. In India it is the
sacred flower of Siva.

The trunk is smooth, but the branches are thorny. The light green,
compound leaves are feather-like, made up of tiny, three-fourth inch long,
leaflets. The colorful gaudy flowers appear on the tips of branches in
racemes, similar to the Royal Poinciana. The long blooming season
continues through spring, summer and fall. Individual flowers have five,
crepy, scarlet petals that are edged in yellow, with conspicuously long red
stamens and a pistil, up to two and a half inches long, projecting from the
center. The seed pods which follow the bloom are long and flat, often
exceeding four inches. The small seeds are sometimes used in necklaces.

see color page 79

This is a very fast growing tree in a variety of soils, demanding only a sunny location in a relatively warm area. (Growing as far north as Orlando, it may withstand light frost.) Salt tolerance is poor, or at best fair. It is semi-deciduous in cool weather. The Dwarf Poinciana is propagated by seeds. (Place the seeds in warm water, let them soak for twenty-four hours and plant them in sandy soil; transfer to pots when first leaves appear.) The tree may be pruned to shape, to remove dead wood or shorten the shoots after flowering.

In the landscape, these are conspicuous, ornamental trees, used as a tall, untrimmed hedge, filler shrub or specimen tree. *Poinciana flava* is a variety similar in habit but bearing yellow flowers.

Earleaf Acacia

Earleaf Acacia   *Acacia auriculaeformis*

These tropical evergreen trees of the Legume family, like many of the other six hundred or more species of Acacia, are native in Australia. Several varieties are widely grown in Florida and California and many others grow throughout the warm areas of the world. All the Acacias produce flowers, some in ball form, others in spikes. In Australia they are called Wattles. Early settlers built houses of "Wattle and Daub", a wall woven with Acacia branches and covered with mud. The Shittim wood of the Bible, used in the Ark of the Covenant and the Tabernacle, was Acacia wood. It is said to have been used for Christ's "crown of thorns"; the Acacia is called Thorn Tree in Africa. Historically, it has been used in many rituals; a branch is placed inside the coffin at Masonic funerals.

The *A. auriculaeformis* is well suited to the southern half of Florida. It grows to thirty-five feet or more, with slender branches which form a dense crown. The grayish green, leaf like, flattened stems, to eight inches long, are slender, blade-like and curved, resembling a simple leaf.

In spring, bright yellow flowers are borne in clusters on short spikes. They have a pleasant fragrance but it is elusive; sometimes it is quite strong, and at other times imperceptible. Following the bloom are twisted seed pods, four inches long, containing flat, black seeds. The seeds are fastened to the pod by a yellowish filament.

Earleaf Acacia grows rapidly in almost any type soil, in a frost free area with full sun. Its salt tolerance is too low for seaside lawns and it will not withstand severe pruning. The branches are brittle and may break in high winds. Propagation is by seeds or cuttings of half-ripened wood with a heel. Seed germination may be hastened by placing the seeds in hot water and allowing them to cool and soak for twelve to forty-eight hours.

see color page 80

22

Its drought resistance makes Earleaf Acacia an excellent tree for street planting where water is scarce. Spectacular when in bloom, it is used as a hedge or a specimen tree in the garden.

A. macracantha is a smaller tree (to twenty feet), native in Mexico and South America. Its branches have sharp, two inch long spines and tiny, bright green, bipinnate leaflets. Golden yellow, ball-shaped flowers appear in spring, either in clusters or singly.

Floss Silk Tree

Floss Silk Tree   *Chorisia speciosa*

  This very unusual, large, ornamental tree from Brazil and Argentina is named for L. L. Choris, an artist with a scientific expedition led by Otto Van Kotzebue. *Speciosa* means "beautiful", an apt description of this small cousin of the Bombax.

  The most striking characteristic of the Floss Silk Tree is its uncharacteristic behavior. No two specimens seem to be alike. Flowers may be crimson, white, pink, or rosy to purple-hued, but seeds from a tree of one color may produce a tree that bears flowers of any of the other colors. (*Chorisia insignia*, introduced but rarely seen in Florida, has yellow flowers blotched with brown).

  The five-petalled flowers, three or more inches across, are mildly fragrant and appear on Florida trees in the fall, usually from October to December.

24

see color page 63

The upright tree, reaching heights of forty feet or more, has an open crown made up of sprawling, angular limbs covered with alternate, compound, dark green, toothed, lanceolate leaves; the leaves usually fall before the blooms appear. The massive trunk and limbs are usually covered with thick thorns that fall off some trees with age. However, here the Floss Silk tree displays another variable; some specimens never produce any thorns. The pear-shaped, capsular fruit is filled with silky floss, which is similar to that of the Bombax and Kapok trees, and which also has been used for pillow stuffing.

Except for their disdain of salt, Floss Silk trees are not fussy as to soil type, and once established, do not require copious watering. Although they can withstand a short period of freezing temperature, they are tropical enough to prefer a frost free area in full sun. They can be pruned to shape or to remove dead branches. They are usually propagated by air layering as cuttings are difficult to root and few trees ever set seeds in Florida.

If you have a lot of room, are looking for a fast-growing tree, and don't mind being surprised by the color of the flowers you get, this is a choice specimen tree. It is truly spectacular when in bloom – whatever the color!

25

Flowering Dogwood

Flowering Dogwood   *Cornus florida*

This small, graceful tree is well known to most people, and found on fertile, well drained soils under hardwoods from Maine to central Florida and Texas.

A deciduous, horizontal branching tree, it can grow twenty to thirty feet tall, with a spread that may be nearly equal to its height. Its broad, rounded crown has slender brown branches on a comparatively short trunk, with brownish gray bark. The bark develops deep furrows on very old trunks; the trunks can grow to as much as eighteen inches in diameter, but in Florida such size is not common. The wood is heavy, very hard, close grained, and is light brown tinged with red.

The leaves, to six inches, are opposite on the twig, oval, thick, pointed at each end, and veined from midrib to margin. They are bright green on the upper surface, lighter beneath and, especially in northern climates, become brilliantly colored in autumn.

Greenish yellow flowers in dense clusters are surrounded by four large, white, petal-like bracts. Fall fruit is scarlet and shiny, one-half inch across, fleshy with a bony seed.

see color page 60

26

The Dogwood grows moderately fast in fertile, well drained soil. Good drainage is very important. It prefers light shade but will thrive in full sun with good soil, especially in northern and upper central Florida. It can withstand considerable drought once established, but has no salt tolerance. It is easily propagated from mature wood cuttings, by layering or grafting. It is subject to leaf disease and trunk borer problems.

In landscaping, the Dogwood is used as a specimen tree, in groups under pine trees, or for street planting. They are exceptionally beautiful when the woods are glorious with them in bloom or fruit, or in fall color.

Nurseries offer numerous varieties. Cherokee Chief has deep pink flowers; Cloud 9 is a white flowering variety, and Welch Jr. Miss has large, pink flowers. (The pink ones appear to need more cold than the white native variety and do not do as well, especially in the warmer areas of the state.)

Frangipani

Frangipani
Pagoda Tree
Temple Tree

Plumeria accuminata

Though native to tropical America from Mexico to Venezuela and the West Indies, the *Plumeria* has been widely cultivated for centuries in India, Asia, and almost anywhere in the world where the weather is warm. Almost as universal has been its use for planting around temples and burying grounds, hence the common name Temple Tree. Its fragrant flowers are a source of perfume and are used for leis in Hawaii.

This picturesque tree can reach twenty feet but is usually smaller. The comparatively few, stiff, non-tapering, thick, forking branches contain a toxic milky sap which will stain clothing. The tree is bare during the winter; in spring leaf clusters appear at the ends of the rather soft, stubby branches. Alternate dark green leaves may be sixteen inches long and up to four inches wide, with prominent marginal veins. The five thick, velvety, waxy, long-lasting petals of the flower overlap like a pinwheel.

The Mexican Frangipani, *P. acutifolia*, has white, yellow centered blossoms. Another white flowering variety, *P. obtusa* is sold as Singapore Frangipani. The darker, Rhododendron-like leaves are more oblong, more numerous, and remain on the tree all year. The yellow-centered white flowers are larger than the common variety and are highly scented. *P. rubra* was obviously named for its red hue; however, according to some authorities they may be pink, red, purple or even white or yellow. This makes for difficulty in identification, but that may be left to the botanists. The home gardener will simply recognize the white Singapore as a distinguishably different relative – and choose "cousins" simply on the basis of color preference.

see color page 52

In early spring, blooms appear near the branch ends even before the flush of leaf growth, and continue through the summer in masses of terminal clusters.

Frangipani is a showy tree, good as a specimen tree or for background planting with evergreen shrubs. It prefers fertile, sandy loam soil, full sun for maximum bloom, and a frost free area. Its salt tolerance is good and it is easily propagated from cuttings. The preferred method of some people is to cut out a section of branch, and leave it in a dry place for weeks or months before planting. Perhaps it is this ability to produce roots after such treatment that allows the *Plumeria* to weather long periods of drought.

29

Geiger Tree

Geiger Tree
Geranium Tree
Kou

Cardia sebestena

This beautiful, tender, evergreen tree is a native Floridian. Though rather rare now in the wild, it is a native to Dade and Monroe counties. It is becoming popular in the Palm Beach area and southward and can now be found in many nurseries specializing in rare tropical plants. It grows to twenty-five feet in height, with one of the largest specimens growing at the former home of Captain John Geiger in Key West. John Audubon gave the tree its common name when, as a guest of Captain Geiger, he painted many Florida birds. One bird is portrayed roosting in the Geiger tree, surrounded by the colorful flowers. He probably had ample opportunity to observe this, as the tree flowers almost continuously in South Florida.

The brilliant orange-scarlet blooms are two inches long and grow in terminal geranium-like clusters. Individual flowers are tube shaped, having five to seven frilled, crepy lobes with short yellow stamens in the throat. The edible fruit, which matures all year, is white, egg-shaped, reaches one and one-half inches in length, and usually has a single seed.

The tree is host to the Geiger Beetle which seems to feed exclusively on the Geiger tree, seeming to cause it no great harm. It is a colorful, jewel-like little insect that can usually be found under the leaves.

Several qualities make this an ideal landscaping plant in the southern half of the state. Unlike many flowering trees, it tolerates salt, so it is a good seaside tree. Being native to the Keys, it grows (slowly) in limestone or almost solid rock, so it is not particular as to soil type. Best of all, it requires very little water. In any landscape where temperatures remain above freezing, this is an ideal tree, whether near the ocean, as a specimen in the home garden, in parks, or as a street tree.

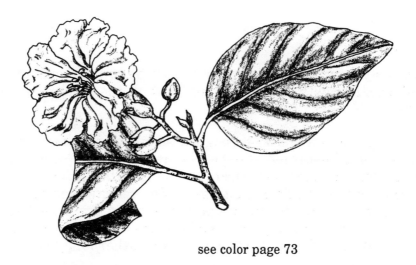

see color page 73

Golden Rain Tree

Golden Rain Tree
China Tree

Koelreuteria paniculata

The name *Koelreuteria* honors Joseph G. Koelreuter (1733 – 1806), professor of natural history at Karlsruhe.

Though this handsome import from China and Japan is deciduous, it offers some kind of ornamentation during most seasons of the year. In May it produces yellow flowers. These are followed by colorful, papery pods that resemble Japanese lanterns. Before falling, the leaves turn yellow; then the "lanterns" turn brown to become seed pods, and hang on far into the winter.

The bright green, bipinnate leaves, up to one and a half feet long, consist of seven to fifteen opposite leaflets, plus one at the end. The leaflets are four inches or more long, ovate-lanceolate, coarsely toothed, notched, and sharply pointed. The numerous flowers grow in panicles, a foot or more long, above the foliage. The bright yellow, pointed petals are deep red at the base, and the pale stamens are tipped with red. The puffed up, bladdery, two-inch long capsules that follow the bloom period may be deep pink to red. Often yellow flowers and red seed pods may be seen on the tree at the same time.

see color page 52

The Golden Rain Tree sometimes reaches thirty feet or more but is a fairly slow grower. However, it is easily cultivated in loamy, well-drained soil. It needs full sun, but makes few other demands and requires little or no maintenance. It is sufficiently cold hardy to withstand winters in any part of Florida; it is very drought tolerant; it is fairly salt tolerant. (It would not withstand frequent bombardment with sea spray, but back from the beach it can be grown in seaside communities.)

Propagation is by root-cuttings or seed, sown as soon as ripe, in sandy soil. In landscaping, it is used as a street tree, or a specimen shade tree.

Golden Shower Tree

Golden Shower Tree

Pudding Pipe Tree

Indian Laburnum

Cassia fistula

Originating in India, this tree is sometimes called Indian Laburnum. While there are several hundred species in the *Cassia* genus (several of which have been introduced into Florida), the most widely cultivated one is the *Cassia fistula*, or Golden Shower.

It is a stately, tree, semi-deciduous, and reaching thirty feet in a short time if grown in fertile, sandy loam soil in full sun. The leaves are large — up to a foot long with eight to sixteen bright green, smooth, compound leaflets, two inches wide and two to six inches long. The tree, which can be pruned to shape, grows naturally into a graceful upright form, with wide, spreading branches, an open crown, and smooth gray bark.

In spring the leaves are often hidden by the cascades of yellow flowers, which extend along the limbs in grape-like clusters to a foot or more in length. Seen in late afternoon sun, they seem to glow; so bright are they that even when carried indoors they appear to generate a brilliance from within. The golden yellow blossoms are pea-like in form with five petals. In the center are long, curving stamens and a pistil which develops into a long, black, round pod to two feet or more long, and contains toxic beans. The pods contain a sticky brown substance which holds the seeds separate. The pulp is sometimes added to tobacco in India, where the tree is also known as the Pudding Pipe Tree. The golden shower tree is propagated by seeds.

Cassia fistula has little or no salt tolerance, and requires above freezing temperatures. However, it is extremely tolerant of dry weather. That, and its beauty, make it a very desirable addition to the Florida scene.

34

see color back cover

35

Jacaranda

Jacaranda
Fern Tree

Jacaranda acutaifolia
Jacaranda mimosifolia

This tree, called Caroba in its native Brazil, is one of Florida's most spectacular. Lilacs may herald the coming of spring for our northern neighbors, but in Florida a large Jacaranda tree covered with cool lavender blue flowers is a scene unsurpassed. There is even beauty when the petals have dropped, creating a carpet of blue on the ground beneath.

In Brazil the Indians use the leaves, and in Panama the bark, for treatment of skin diseases. Natives in Venezuela and Columbia use it for medicinal purposes also. In South Africa and in California it is frequently used for street planting.

see color page 58

The Jacaranda is a large deciduous tree, to forty feet, with upright spreading branches and light gray bark. Opposite leaves are usually two pinnate, bright green and feathery. They grow up to eighteen inches long, with sharply pointed, tiny, fern-like leaflets which fall in early winter.

Flowers appear primarily in spring before the new leaf growth, but may be seen throughout the summer in lesser quantity. The tree is covered with masses of soft, violet-blue trumpet shaped blossoms, two inches long by one and a half inches across, growing in great loose clusters. These are followed by round, flat, woody pods filled with light brown seeds encased in a tissue paper-like covering. Growth is moderately rapid in fertile, sandy loam soil with good drainage and full sun. It is propagated by seeds. It can withstand short periods of freezing temperatures, is relatively insect free, and requires little attention once established.

Except near the beach, for its salt tolerance is poor, it is a very desirable tree for parkway planting, shade tree or specimen tree in a large garden.

Jerusalem Thorn

Jerusalem Thorn   *Parkinsonia aculeata*

Native in tropical America, this attractive, fern-like, small tree is widely used by landscape architects around the world where the climate is warm enough to accommodate it. It is named for John Parkinson, the English botanist (1567 – 1650).

Although Jerusalem is a most unlikely locale for this tree, the "thorn" part of its common name is easily seen. It grows to thirty feet, a graceful, drooping, deciduous with green bark and feathery, pendulous green branches armed with thorns to one inch long. Although bare of tiny leaves for a short time, the green trunk, branches, and branchlets give the illusion of an evergreen. The trunk is prone to be crooked unless it is staked when young and trained to grow straight. The yellowish leaves are very tiny and produced on flat leaf stems. Bright yellow flowers appear periodically, but more profusely in early spring. They are fragrant, small (an inch or less), and are composed of five crinkly petals, one often having a streak or blotch of red. They hang in loose clusters and are followed by slender pods, to five inches long.

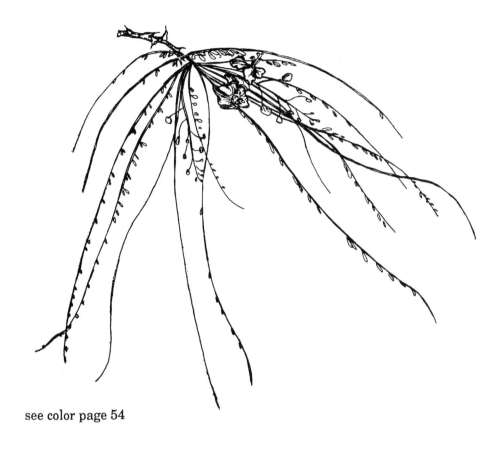

see color page 54

Parkinsonia grows moderately fast in fertile, sandy loam soil. It will grow in either full sun or partial shade; it will withstand a few degrees of frost, is very tolerant of drought, and though it prefers an inland location, it can be grown near the sea. It is propagated by seeds or hardwood cuttings. Large trees are difficult to transplant, and should be root pruned before moving.

Parkinsonia is highly recommended for small home planting, or against buildings where its transparent lacy effect will not hide the architecture. It is also used in courtyards, patios, and as a parkway tree.

Parkinsonia terreyana is native in Arizona and Texas. It is a smaller tree (to twenty-five feet) with fewer leaflets, similar bright yellow flowers, and three-inch long seed pods.

Lignum Vitae

Lignum Vitae   *Guaiacum sanctum*

One of very few native Florida trees with showy flowers, this attractive tree will attain a height of thirty feet. There are about eight species of Guaiacum in Florida, the Caribbean, and Central America. Lignum Vitae's lovely blue blossom is the national flower of Jamaica. The common name means "tree of life", and refers to the medicinal uses of the wood, bark, fruit and flowers. The tree's curative properties were recognized by visitors to the New World as early as the sixteenth century. The heartwood is also highly prized, being extra-ordinarily heavy, hard, and oily. The oily sap dries out very slowly, allowing the wood to retain its resiliency. It was once commonly used for bowling balls, mallet heads, bowls, and in shipbuilding, primarily for propeller shafts. The usefulness of this tree to man has contributed to its downfall — very few specimens are left in Florida and Lignum Vitae is now a protected species here.

see color front cover

Lignum Vitae is a small, ornamental, evergreen tree with fine textured, dense foliage which forms a round, compact crown. Its bright green leaves are pinnate, with two to four pairs of oval to broad obovate leaflets, each up to two inches long.

In late spring, large clusters of velvety blue flowers, up to one-half inch in length, appear at the branch tips. Yellow-orange fruit often appears at the same time, making the tree very colorful. The fruit is attractive, though small, being less than an inch long. It is a strongly angled, heart-shaped capsule, with a leathery skin, red pulp, and dark brown seeds. *G. officinale* is similar to *G. sanctum*, but its leaves are round, rather than oval, and its fruit has bright red seeds. Both species are referred to by the common name, Lignum Vitae, and both grow in Florida.

Lignum Vitae has many positive traits for Florida gardens, namely, excellent salt and drought tolerance, and a preference for the nutrient-poor, limestone soil found in coastal regions of the state. However, it is an extremely slow growing tree, and will grow only in the southernmost part of the state, since it requires a frost-free climate. It makes an excellent specimen or shade tree, ideal for small residential gardens in south Florida.

40

41

Lipstick Tree

Annatto
Arnotto
Lipstick Tree

Bixa orellana

This is a tropical American tree, commonly found in South Florida, the West Indies and from Mexico through South America. It is often grown as a shrub but will develop into a tree, to twenty feet, with a dense, rounded, bush crown and a short slender trunk with fibrous bark.

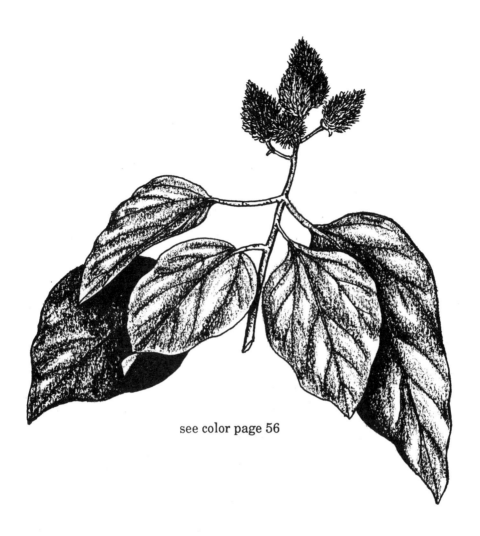

see color page 56

The large leaves are alternate on the branches, heart shaped, dark green and growing to about seven inches. They are prominently veined with wavy margins and pointed tips. In early spring, flowers are borne in heavy clusters. The pale pink, white, or rose colored blossoms are two inches across and consist of five petals surrounding a mass of stamens. The conspicuously ornamental seed pods which follow are two inches long, and covered with soft deep red spines which turn brown as they dry. The pod splits to reveal many small seeds coated with a light red substance which provides the annatto dye widely used for coloring cheese, butter, and other foods. Ancient warriors and tribesmen in Africa have used the dye for color on their bodies. Parts of the plant are used for medicinal purposes.

This tree grows rapidly in fertile, sandy loam soil. It needs full sun and above freezing temperatures. Its poor salt tolerance precludes it as a beach tree, and it is less drought resistant than some of the other flowering trees. But, in a landscape where its conditions are met, it is an attractive accent tree. The seed pods are extremely attractive and are often used in flower arrangements.

Loquat

Loquat   *Eriobotrya japonica*

This native of China and Japan got its name from Greek words *erion* (wool) and *botrys* (cluster). The name was well chosen for this plant, with its bunches of felty fruit stalks and fruit. It is a handsome small evergreen which grows to about thirty feet with short trunk and wide spreading branches.

The decorative leaves are thick, stiff and obovate, a foot long and three to five inches wide. They are shiny and dark green above, rusty tomentose beneath, and deeply veined.

In autumn tiny, creamy white, fragrant flowers appear on wooly panicles. Fruit is pear shaped, yellow or orange, up to two inches long with two to four dark brown seeds, ripening in late winter or early spring.

The tree will withstand lower temperatures than its fruit or flowers, so the fruit will mature only in warm regions. The fruit is delicious eaten fresh or used in preserves.

Once established, the Loquat grows rapidly in any type of soil, but its preference would be a light loamy soil, with a heavy mulch of leaves, compost, or peat. It is a tree that makes few demands. It can weather a few degrees of freezing temperature. It has good salt tolerance. It can withstand drought. It likes full sun, but tolerates some shade.

see color page 60

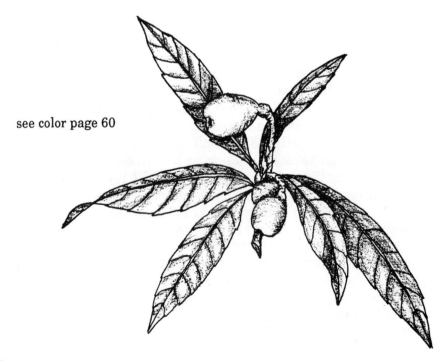

44

Although it may be propagated by seed, the fruit of seedling trees may be inferior, so it is not the best method. Improved varieties are grafted on seedling stock. Some of them are Advance, Oliver, Wolfe, Gold Nugget, and Tanaka.

The loquat is popular in landscaping as a specimen tree in the garden or patio. It is excellent for espaliering or as a potted subject because of its limited size, interesting growth habit and pleasing appearance. Since all the above are enough to recommend it, edible fruit must be considered a bonus!

Mahoe

Hibiscus tiliaceus

Mahoe
Sea Hibiscus
Tree Hibiscus

    This tree probably came from the Old World tropics, but it is now native to the coastal regions and the Keys. A sprawling, gnarled tree, it grows to twenty-five feet in marshes along the seashore, where its many long branches may form an almost impenetrable thicket. Of creeping habit, the branches twist along the ground and must be supported; however, they can be pruned and trained into almost any desired shape. The rough, blotched bark is light gray. The trunk, sometimes as much as two feet in diameter, is often twisted picturesquely.

    The large, alternate, heart shaped, leathery leaves are dark green above, lighter and downy beneath, and are prominently veined. This typical hibiscus flower has five overlapping petals and a central column, and may be four inches across. The blossoms appear on long, downy stalks of new growth, from June through September. When they open in the morning, they are clear, bright yellow, with a maroon center. They change to orange later in the day, and become dark red before they finally fall. However, there appear to be variations in the timing of the color change among individual blossoms, and often the tree displays all three colors at the same time. The small seed pods are silky and cone shaped. When mature, they split into five sections, revealing small, brown, kidney-shaped seeds.

see color page 69

46

Propagation is by seeds, air-layering or cuttings. Some consider it a messy tree, as flowers fall constantly. It may be affected by snow scales on the stems, and chewing insects occasionally attack the leaves. Also, it breaks easily in high winds. While the above characteristics may make it undesirable for many gardens, it has its place. Unlike many flowering trees, it has a high tolerance for salt. This makes it an excellent choice for the beach garden, where it is most attractive, either trained on an arbor or as a specimen in the yard. Given full sun, moist, alkaline, well-drained soil, and a frost free climate, it grows rapidly.

Some nurseries may call this tree a Cuban Bast. However, there is some confusion here, and many authorities give that common name to a related species, *H. elatus*, which has narrow petals that are separated and do not overlap, pinwheel fashion, as do the Mahoe petals. Both progressively change their colors.

Some Leaf Forms

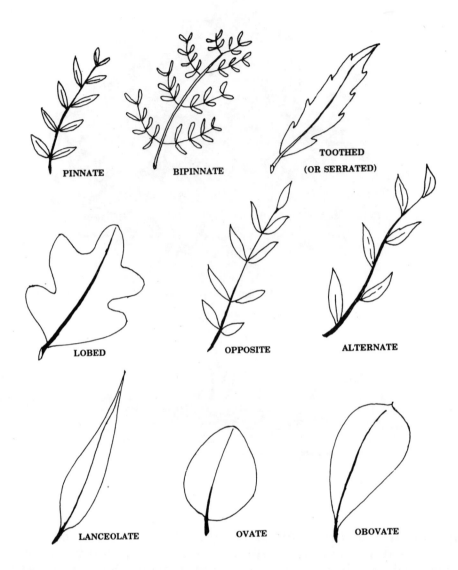

PINNATE

BIPINNATE

TOOTHED
(OR SERRATED)

LOBED

OPPOSITE

ALTERNATE

LANCEOLATE

OVATE

OBOVATE

All of the following color illustrations (and those on the cover), plus the many pen and pencil sketches of trees and blossoms throughout this book were done by the author. Some were done years ago, others quite recently.

The cover illustrations are:

Front cover – Bombax (page 14) and Lignum Vitae (page 40).

Back cover – Golden Shower (page 34).

The number on each illustration is the page number of corresponding descriptive text.

108 POINCIANA

8 AFRICAN TULIP

94 PINK TRUMPET

120 SILVER TRUMPET

51

28 FRANGIPANI

32 GOLDEN RAIN TREE

92 ORCHID TREE

53

38   JERUSALEM THORN

118   SILK OAK

96 PITCH APPLE

42 LIPSTICK TREE

10 ANGEL'S TRUMPET

98 POINSETTIA

126 TAMARIND

59

26 FLOWERING DOGWOOD

44 LOQUAT

12 BEAUTY LEAF

102 QUEEN'S CRAPE MYRTLE

110 SAUCER MAGNOLIA

84 MARLBERRY

62

24 FLOSS SILK

63

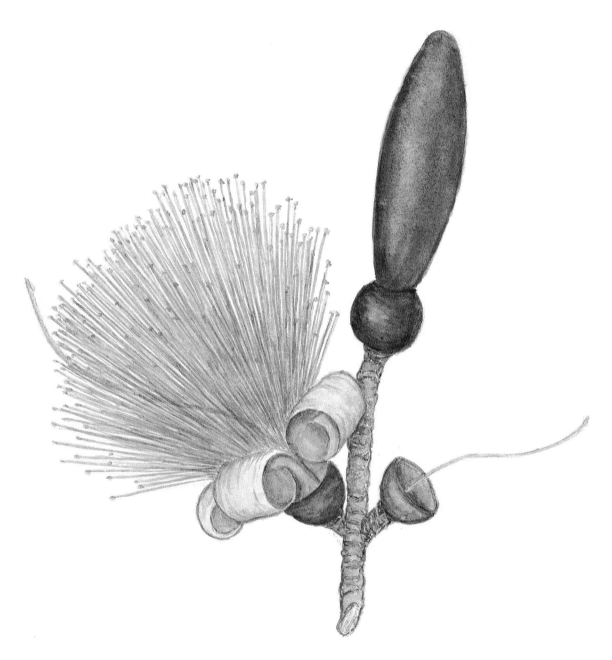

116 SHAVING BRUSH

128   WOMAN'S TONGUE

16   BOTTLE BRUSH

100   POWDER PUFF

134   YELLOW POINCIANA

66

114 SCHEFFLERA

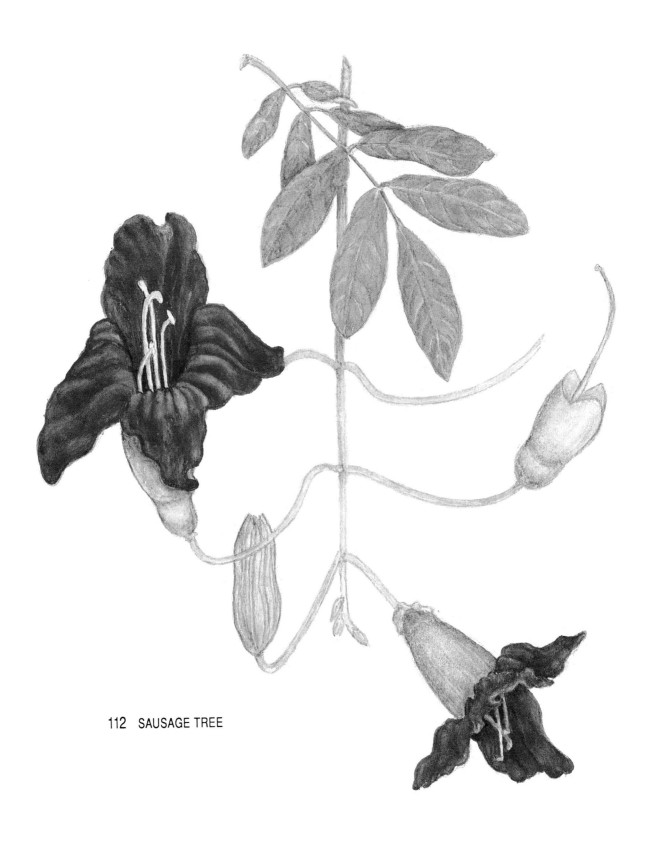

112 SAUSAGE TREE

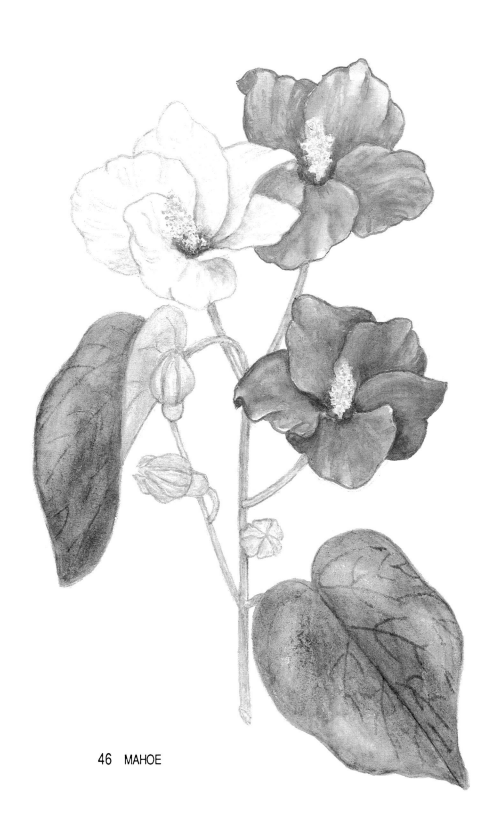

46 MAHOE

122 SOUTHERN MAGNOLIA

70

136   YELLOW SILK COTTON

86   MEXICAN ROSE

124 SWEET ACACIA

30 GEIGER TREE

73

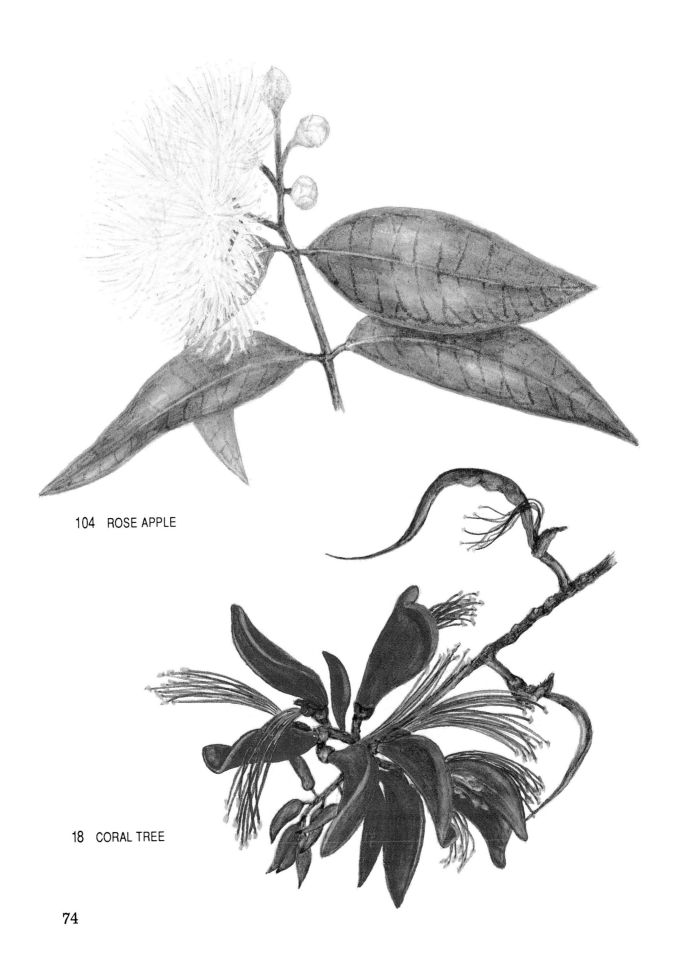

104 ROSE APPLE

18 CORAL TREE

74

82 MALAY APPLE

130   YELLOW ELDER

76

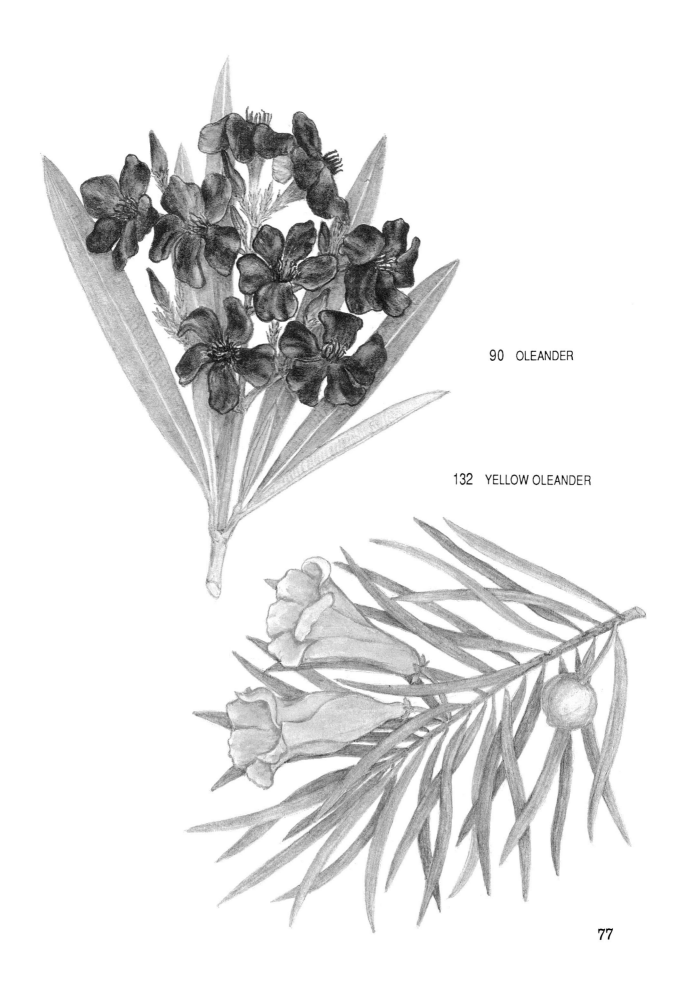

90 OLEANDER

132 YELLOW OLEANDER

106   ROSE OF VENEZUELA

20　DWARF POINCIANA

22 EARLEAF ACACIA

88 MIMOSA

80

About Names

In a scientific work, the forty-eight trees described and pictured here would be arranged in a quite different sequence. However, the unscientific aim of this book is not a lofty one. It is simply to allow the layman (possibly a person who has moved to Florida from a totally different climate) to "browse". It offers a nodding acquaintance with some attractive and interesting warm weather trees available for adding beauty, color, and shade to the reader's immediate environment.

For botanists, the trees would be arranged by family, with related species grouped together; our Jacaranda would be somewhere near the Sausage Tree since both belong to the vast BIGNONIACEAE family — a fact of no great importance to one who simply wants a Jacaranda tree for its lovely blue flowers. With this in mind, and for the sake of brevity, "family" has been omitted.

We could have alphabetized the trees by species names. If you had some knowledge of botany this might lead you to the tree you seek. Or perhaps not, had you looked for Malay Apple under "S" for *Syzygium malaccense* when it might be found under "E" for *Eugenia malaccensis*; among botanists, there has long been disagreement in the area of taxonomy.

In the end, the trees were arranged alphabetically (more or less!) according to their common names. Of course, this way perhaps leads to greater chaos, since any given plant (or fish, or bird) may be called by one common name in one area, but by a quite different one in another locale. One man's Powder Puff Tree may be another man's Flame Bush. That is why Latin names are used in the scientific community. At least *most* of the time, two scientists can be sure they are talking about the same organism. Thus, to allay at least some confusion, species names as well as common names are included. Also the etymology of some scientific names is fun, and sometimes reveals something about the tree or its history.

Arranging the trees alphabetically by common name is then, admittedly, rather haphazard. However, that might just be the arrangement of the trees you encounter when you visit your local nursery. And wandering through your local nursery is the activity that it is hoped this book will encourage. Now that you have been introduced to these forty-eight trees, visit your local nurseryman and browse! He may or may not be well versed in scientific nomenclature; he may very well know still other common (local) names for the trees shown here. But if he operates an established Florida nursery he can almost surely impart valuable knowledge and will be able to tell you if a particular tree will grow well in your neighborhood. Get to know him (or her)!

Malay Apple

Malay Apple
Mountain Apple

Eugenia malaccensis
syn. *Syzygium malaccense*

An outstanding flowering tree which is native to India and Malaya, this tree was brought to Jamaica in 1793 by Captain Bligh aboard the Providence, along with fruit from Tahiti. It was brought to Hawaii by early settlers in sailing canoes, and was the only fruit they had until Europeans introduced others. Natives considered it sacred, and used the wood for temple idols. This tree is closely related to the Rose Apple, *E. jambos*. Some scientists disagree about the scientific name of the Malay Apple, so the name *Syzygium* is also widely used.

Under favorable conditions, the Malay Apple will attain thirty feet in height, with dense evergreen foliage near the top. Bark is smooth, mottled gray. Dark green, shiny leaves are large, thick and smooth, oblong to obovate in shape, prominently veined, reaching twelve inches in length.

In early spring reddish purple flowers, reaching two inches across, are borne on the trunk and main branches. The tufts of red stamens, which are the most noticeable part, exceed in length the petals which enclose them. As the flowers fall, a bright red carpet is laid on the ground. The crimson, egg-shaped fruit, to three inches long, has a large seed in the center. The fruit looks much like an apple, with white, crisp, juicy flesh that can be eaten raw or used in preserves or to make wine.

Easily cultivated, the Malay Apple will grow rapidly in moist, fertile soil, full sun and a frost free area. Its salt tolerance is poor. It may be propagated by seed or by cuttings. In landscaping, it is used as a windbreak or as a specimen shade tree.

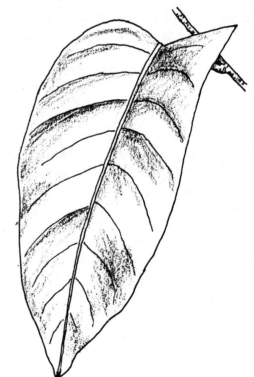

see color page 75

82

Marlberry

Marlberry   *Ardisia paniculata*

Native in southern Florida, the West Indies and Mexico, this small evergreen tree is widely planted in the gardens of South Florida and the Keys. Its rather diminutive size (twenty feet) makes it popular where there is limited space. The name *Ardisia* is derived from *ardis*, "a point", and refers to pointed petals.

Alternate, simple, dark green, glossy, leathery, seven-inch leaves make up the dense foliage. Blooms appear throughout the year, but more profusely in spring or early summer. The small flowers are white when opened, and occur in panicles at the branch tips. When in bud they are rose tinged. The small, pinkish-red berries turn shiny black when mature. This means that frequently the tree is adorned with blooms in two colors and fruit at the same time.

The Marlberry grows moderately fast in fertile, sandy, acid soil and full sun. It will withstand light frost and has good salt tolerance. It may be pruned to shape and to remove dead branches. Propagation is by seeds sown in late winter or early spring, or by cuttings. (Nurseries insure root growth of cuttings by using half mature wood over bottom heat.)

see color page 62

84

Marlberry trees are useful in landscaping as a hedge, foundation plant, or group planting, or as a specimen tree. *A. crispa*, native in Malaya and China, is a fast-growing shrub (to seven feet) with glossy green leaves and white flowers in clusters. It is often grown as a potted plant in greenhouses, and is valued for its abundant crop of long lasting, scarlet berries.

Mexican Rose

Mexican Rose
Hydrangea Tree
Pink Ball

Dombeya wallichii

This tropical evergreen tree is native in Madagascar and India. A vigorous upright tree, it grows to thirty feet with wide, spreading branches forming a compact, rounded crown. The *Dombeyas*, of which there are many species, are named in honor of a French botanist, Joseph Dombey.

The foliage of this tree is so dense that it often partially hides the showy flowers. The leaves are alternate, palmately veined, heart shaped with a point on each side. They are large leaves, up to a foot long, toothed, bright green above and velvety whitish green beneath. These are winter blooming trees, usually at their best at Christmas time. The many pink flowers form large, dense balls, which hang at the end of long, downy pedicles. Each floret has five petals, with stamens extending from a short tube in the center. When the flowers fade, they turn brown and remain on the tree for a long time. For best appearance, the faded flowers should be cut off. The fruit is capsular.

see color page 72

86

This is a rapid grower, in fertile, sandy, loam soil, with full sun and no freezing weather. It is not very tolerant of either salt or excessive drought. Because of its rapid growth, it needs frequent pruning. In landscaping it is used as a specimen tree, or when pruned makes a good shrub for screening or as a foundation plant.

Popular varieties are *D. ocutangula*, a small tree or shrub with reddish or white flowers (sometimes labelled "tropical snowball"), *D. natalensis*, a shrub to eight feet with pink flowers. *D. cayeuxii* is a hybrid and produces pink flowers.

Mimosa

Mimosa
Silk Tree

Albizzia julibrissin

Native from Iran to Japan, this small deciduous tree is very popular in the southern U.S. It usually has multiple trunks, and attains a height of thirty feet, with wide, spreading branches which form an umbrella shaped shade tree. In March or April fern-like, feathery foliage is produced. Leaves are bipinnate, to ten inches long, composed of bright green, oval leaflets to one-half inch long, arranged opposite on the common stem. Leaflets fold together at night.

see color page 80

In early summer, the tree is covered with a profusion of pinkish flower heads resembling powder puffs. The fluffy blossoms are crowded on the tips of branches for a long period. Seed pods are then formed, which reach six inches in length; they are strap shaped and yellowish brown in color.

The Mimosa grows rapidly in almost all soils in the South, in sun or partial shade. Hardy, it will survive in sheltered areas as far north as Washington. Salt tolerance is poor, but add it to the list of trees that can withstand dry seasons. No regular pruning is necessary. Propagated by seeds or cuttings. This tree is susceptible to Mimosa wilt. In landscaping, it is used as a specimen tree, shade tree, or for avenue planting.

Oleander

Oleander   *Nerium oleander*

This well known and popular evergreen tree (or shrub) is native from the Mediterranean region to Japan. The name *Nerium* is derived from *neros*, meaning humid, which describes the kind of environment this tree would probably choose. However, it is very adaptable, as it is one of our more drought tolerant trees. Globular in shape with dense foliage, they sometimes reach twenty feet in height. Though most often seen as clumps with branches coming off at ground level, nurserymen are training Oleanders into single trunk trees. In either form they are spectacular when in bloom.

Dull, dark green leaves are opposite, or whorled in threes and fours. The stiff, pointed, oblong-lanceolate leaves grow to eight inches.

There are several points in its favor: it isn't particular about soil; it will grow rather rapidly in almost any type that is well-drained and in full sun. It is hardy. It will tolerate sea spray, high winds, city conditions, and even short periods of freezing weather. (It may die back but will sprout from the roots.) It is easily propagated from cuttings, sometimes in water, or by air-layering at any time of year. It can be pruned in spring to control height.

see color page 77

90

Except for the Oleander caterpillar, which can be controlled with Lindane, it is free of pests or disease. It blooms periodically year round, as clusters of funnel-form blossoms appear at the branch tips. Colors range from white to shades of yellow, pink and purple. "Trade names" at the nursery will identify the hue. With little attention it can be a beautiful addition to the landscape as a specimen, street tree, informal hedge, screen or tub plant in the beach yard or the park.

However, it has one very bad feature. All parts of this plant are extremely poisonous. People have become ill, or even died, from inhaling smoke from burning the wood, from eating wieners roasted on the cut stems, or from eating food touched by the blossoms that were used as table decorations. Dispose of cuttings with caution and refrain from planting it where there are children!

Orchid Tree

Orchid Tree
Hong Kong Orchid
Poor Man's Orchid

Bauhinia blakeana

The *Bauhinia* was named in honor of John and Caspar Bauhin, famous Swiss botanists. These small, but spectacular, evergreen flowering trees are native to China and India. The *blakeana* variety was discovered growing in Hong Kong by a French priest who named it in honor of Sir Henry Blake, governor of Hong Kong around the beginning of this century.

In addition to the *blakeana* there are literally hundreds of other members of the *Bauhinia* genus that grow throughout the warm areas of the world. They include trees, shrubs, and even woody vines. Only botanists may recognize the subtle differences among some of them (and occasionally even botanists have disagreed!)

The home landscaper visiting a Florida nursery will of course have far fewer options, but may choose from several varieties and colors, ranging from white to pink, to reddish and purple. Colors may vary even among some species, and the blooming times also differ with variety.

You may find *B. purpura,* bearing clusters of blooms from September through December, or *B. variegata* (Poor Man's Orchid) which is probably the most common and which blooms from January through March. It loses its leaves while blooming. Also seen is a pure white variety which may be seen labelled *B. variegata candida alba* (or White Mountain Ebony).

But the *blakeana* is perhaps the most spectacular, with its large (five to six inches), fragrant, reddish purple blooms lasting three to four days before fading. They do resemble the blossom of the cattleya orchid. Bright green leaves, to six inches across, are two-lobed, split one third of their length, suggesting the wings of a large moth or, to some, the cloven hoof of an animal. The veins radiate from the stem conjuncture to the margin. The foliage may be shed in spring for a short period.

The tree grows to twenty feet or more, with a slender trunk and spreading, slightly drooping branches (it needs training in its early years for a shapely tree.)

This variety does not appear to produce seeds and must be propagated by air layering or grafting. It grows rapidly in sandy, loam soil if well drained and in full sun. Salt tolerance is fair and it is quite tolerant of drought. While orchid trees are used extensively from Orlando southward, throughout the state, the *blakeana* seems a little less cold hardy than some of the other varieties.

see color page 53

Pink Trumpet

Pink Trumpet
Pink Tecoma
White Cedar

Tabebuia pentaphylla
Tabebuia pallida

Since they resemble the *Stenolobium stans* (*Tecoma stans*), some of the *Tabebuia* were formerly classified as *Tecoma*. Copycats in another way, they are referred to as White Cedar in places where their strong timber, used for interior finishing of houses, is seen to resemble the wood of cedar. The Pink Trumpet tree is native in the West Indies, and Central and South America. It is the national tree of Salvador where it is known as Maquilishuat. Botanists recognize each of a number of pink flowering *Tabebuia* as distinct, and note differences to set apart the various species. However, for the Florida gardener it is probably just as well to leave the nomenclature to the experts; either Pink Trumpet tree will be a welcome addition to the South or Central Florida landscape. (They are not quite as cold hardy as the Silver Trumpet, which has yellow flowers.)

The stiff, bright green leaves grow in groups of three to five leaflets of irregular size, radiating from a common center on a short leaf stalk.

The Pink Trumpet will flower when only two years old. In late winter or early spring, the tree is covered with bloom, looking like one huge bouquet. Colors may be pink, rose, or sometimes white with colored veins. Mildly fragrant, the flowers have a white tube edged with five crinkled, irregular lobes. After the initial burst of bloom, a few may occur throughout the year. The tree is usually bare of leaves when it produces its spring bloom.

see color page 51

94

It will thrive even in poor soil but for best results it should be given fertile, sandy loam in a sunny and frost free location. No pests or diseases are known to attack it, but its salt tolerance is rather poor. Its drought resistance is a plus as Florida becomes ever more water conscious. It can be propagated by cuttings, air-layering or seeds. Many nurseries in southern Florida graft it to Silver Trumpet root stock.

In landscaping, a Pink Trumpet makes an outstanding specimen or background tree.

Pitch Apple

Clusia rosea

Pitch Apple
Autograph Tree
Signature Tree
Balsam Apple

This tender, small, evergreen tree is native in the Florida Keys and the Caribbean. In its natural habitat it usually grows on a host tree and often sends down aerial roots in the manner of a Strangler Fig. A characteristic of its leaves gave it the interesting common names of Autograph and Signature Tree. Its rubbery leaves retain for a long time any scratches made on them. People used to plant them by the front door so that visitors could sign them, leaving a "living calling card."

The opposite leaves are obovate, thick, leathery, stiff, sometimes rolled under at the edges, deep green and glossy above, and lighter green beneath. They grow to eight inches long and nearly as wide with a heavy midvein.

The short trunk has rather smooth bark with oblong raised surfaces. The branches are broad and spreading. It may be pruned to shape.

The unusual, four inch blooms, which appear irregularly but most frequently in late summer, are white with a rosy pink circular stripe and a chartreuse center, looking more artificial than real. The wet looking center produces a sweet, sticky nectar. The fruit is greenish white, pear shaped, to three inches in diameter. The numerous hard, small, oval seeds contain a sticky resin which is used to caulk the seams of boats.

see color page 55

96

The Pitch Apple grows rather slowly, in fertile, sandy loam soil. It prefers full sun but will tolerate some shade. It will not tolerate freezing temperatures. It is drought resistant, and it is not harmed by salt air and salt spray, making it a desirable beach garden tree. Propagation is by seed or air layering.

In its required tropical environment, the Pitch Apple is a good subject for espaliering, as a street tree, foundation shrub or specimen tree.

Poinsettia

Poinsettia   *Euphorbia pulcherrima*

This Christmas flower needs no introduction; it is the one Florida blossom that would be recognized by almost everyone in the country. Native in tropical America and Mexico, it is usually grown as a shrub but will grow to twelve feet if not pruned. Poinsettias are well adapted to Florida and are very widely planted.

Its bright green leaves are oval and tapering, sometimes with pointed lobes; the upper ones are narrow and brilliant red, masquerading as part of the bloom. The true blooms are small, greenish yellow in cymes. The fruit is a three-parted capsule. In south Florida, Poinsettias bloom throughout the winter months. Their blooming time is set according to the number of hours of light in the day, so a brilliant street light nearby may affect it.

Poinsettias grow rapidly in fertile, well drained soil and full sun. Not a plant for the xeriscaped garden, they need to be kept moist. However, they should not be allowed to remain excessively wet for long periods. They require a frost free area and have little salt tolerance.

see color page 59

98

They are easily propagated by cuttings. For compact growth and bloom for the Christmas season, they should be cut back severely before the first of September. The milky juice in the stems could cause a rash in susceptible individuals.

There are many varieties of Poinsettias. White or pink ones are available. (In the nursery they may be labeled *alba* or *rosea*, respectively.) Single types are most frequently seen, but becoming increasingly popular is the double variety, Christmas Star, which is just as easily cultivated, has huge heads, even more brilliant color, and is twice as showy as the single variety.

Powder Puff Tree

Powder Puff Tree
Trinidad Flame Bush

Calliandra guildingii

More than one hundred kinds of *Calliandra* are known. The very apt name is derived from *kallas*, meaning "beauty" and *andros*, meaning "stamens" The powder puff-like flowers appear periodically year round but more profusely in spring. The flowers are greenish white and insignificant; it is the bright red, showy, three-inch long stamens that are so conspicuous. Flat seed pods follow the bloom.

see color page 66

100

This small tropical evergreen tree came from Trinidad. Although often treated as a shrub in South Florida, it will develop into a dense, broad spreading, globose tree. The feathery, bright green leaves are two pinnate with paired two inch leaflets.

Given fertile, sandy, loam soil in a frost free area and in full sun, *Calliandra* grows fairly quickly; it is only moderately tolerant of either salt or extended dry weather, and calcareous soil can present a minor element deficiency. Propagation is by seeds, cuttings, or air-layering. It withstands pruning well, and is very useful and ornamental as an accent or a screen.

There are three other recommended varieties; one of these is *C. haematocephala*, or Redhead Powder Puff. It is of unknown origin, grows to thirty feet, and produces four inch, bright red pompoms from December to April. *C. tweedii* is a shrub from Brazil which grows only six feet tall and has long, showy, purple stamens. It is probably the most cold hardy, reportedly withstanding temperatures as low as 10° to 15° F.

A third variety, also from Brazil, is *C. selloe*, introduced to Florida in 1958 by Edwin Menninger. It too, is a small tree, with fern-like foliage and large heads of red blossoms.

Queen's Crape Myrtle

Queen's Crape Myrtle
Queen of Flowers

Lagerstroemia speciosa

Native from India to Australia, this spectacular tree will attain a height of 60 feet, but in south Florida it usually averages twenty feet. *Lagerstroemis* honors M. Lagerstroem, a Swedish botanist; speciosa in Latin means "pleasing to the eye." In India, where it is called Jarool, it is valued for its tough red timber, which is used in marine building.

The large, rough, deciduous leaves are bright green oblong to ovate. They are four to twelve inches long, resembling huge guava leaves.

The crinkled flowers vary in color from bright pink to purple and appear in late spring and summer. The upright flower spikes, up to two feet long, consist of tubular, frilly, six-petalled blossoms, three inches across. The flower spikes are produced on the current year's growth. Fruit is a woody, berry-like capsule.

see color page 61

102

Crape Myrtles grow rapidly in fertile, sandy loam soil with good drainage and full sun. Although a tender tree, it will withstand a short period of freezing temperature. Salt tolerance is fair. It may be propagated by seed but more often by air layering and cuttings. Crape Myrtle should be pruned when dormant, after the leaves shed in the fall. This promotes new growth (which bears the bloom) and makes for compact growth. The suckers which spring up around the base should be removed. In landscaping, Crape Myrtle is used as a background subject with evergreens, or as a specimen tree in the garden. Though smaller than most "street trees", it is often used to line driveways and parking lots.

The Crape Myrtle shrub *L. indica*, although related, is a far less tropical plant. Though Queen's Crape Myrtle can stand a short period of freezing temperatures, it could never survive the winters that its smaller relatives endure across the southern half of the U. S.

Rose Apple

Rose Apple
Plum Rose

Eugenia jambos
(syn. *Syzygium jambos*)

The Rose Apple is a beautiful ornamental tree which is native to tropical Asia. Its scientific name was given in honor of Prince Eugene of Savoy, who was a patron of botany and horticulture in seventeenth century Austria.

This large evergreen grows to 30 feet or more, and has branches that form a broad, dense crown. Its bark is light brown in color and fissured. Its hard, heavy wood is used for fuel in Asia. The leaves of the Rose Apple are attractive, a dark glossy green above and lighter green underneath. They are opposite, lanceolate, and large, growing to eight inches in length and three in width.

In spring, the conspicuous flowers appear at the ends of branches in clusters to three inches across, opening a few at a time. The petals are greenish white, but are obscured by masses of showy, off-white or yellowish colored stamens which may be up to three inches in length. Pretty, egg-shaped fruit, two inches in diameter, follows the blossom. It may be greenish or yellowish, and is tinged with pink. Its crisp flesh tastes like rose water. The rose fragrance persists even when the fruit is made into preserves.

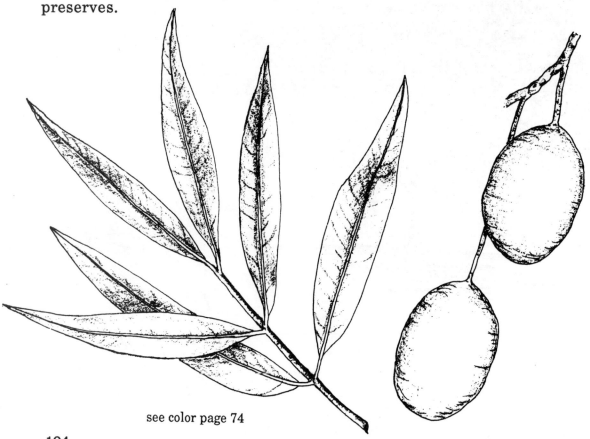

see color page 74

104

While the fruit of the Rose Apple is commonly eaten in Malaysia, it is not as sought after as the fruit of the Malay Apple, to which it is closely related. Other relatives are guava, clove and allspice trees. *E. uniflora*, the Surinam Cherry, is a shrub or tree often used as a hedge in Florida, which bears delicious crimson red fruit. *E. paniculata*, Brush Cherry, is a small, vigorous, Australian tree which is commonly used in landscaping as a sheared accent plant or for foundation planting. There are at least nine species of *Eugenia* which are indigenous to Florida and are considered flowering trees, but they are not commercially available. They typically have smaller flowers than their tropical relatives.

Rose of Venezuela

Rose of Venezuela
Mountain Rose

Brownea capitella
Brownea spp.

The name Brownea is given to at least twenty species of these magnificent flowering trees from South America. While the eleven inch wide blooms of the *B. grandiceps* are perhaps the most spectacular, all are attractive and may be grown in Florida's frost free areas; unfortunately, they have not been widely planted. The first *Brownea* known to have been planted in this country was brought from Trinidad by Dr. George Tyrrell and planted near La Belle, Florida. It was still growing there, near the Caloosahatchee River, fifty years later, and may still be there. The *Brownea* is named for Patrick Brown, an eighteenth century botanist in Jamaica.

Common to all *Brownea* species are bright pink to orange semiglobular flower heads with numerous showy stamens protruding past the blossoms to form a huge glowing ball. In *B. grandiceps* the flower heads resemble *Rhododendron*, with tightly packed pink or red blossoms, and stamens that may be only slightly longer than the petals. In *B. capitella*, the stamens may extend three inches past the flower head and may be so numerous that the somewhat smaller flower head is almost obscured.

Periodically throughout the year, the flowers are produced along main branches, rather than at the stem ends (the term for this is "cauliflorous"). The leathery, pinnate leaves, up to nine inches long, ultimately become dark green. But interestingly, they first appear as a tassel, which unrolls to display a fully grown leaf, splotched with red, purplish-pink, and white. The leaves alone make it an unusual, beautiful tree.

Brownea trees grow fairly quickly in fertile, sandy loam soil, preferably in full sun, and away from the beach; their salt tolerance is low. Propagation is usually by cuttings in pots of sandy peat, in April. Although it may be propagated by seeds, the trees in Florida seem to set seeds only rarely.

B. grandiceps grows to sixty feet or more; *B. capitella* is a somewhat smaller variety and *B. macrophylla* is a climbing shrub, with six-inch wide flowers growing directly on the woody trunk or larger limbs.

Where weather permits, either species of *Brownea* would make an interesting addition to the landscape.

106

see color page 78

107

Royal Poinciana

Royal Poinciana:
Flamboyant
Flame Tree

Delonix regia

Native to Madagascar, this widely planted, tropical, ornamental tree is one of the world's most striking when, from May to July in Florida, it spreads a canopy of scarlet-orange over its branches. A deciduous, wide spreading, umbrella-shaped tree that is often twice as wide as it is high, it will grow to thirty feet or more. The heavy, gnarled trunk and branches of older trees make them picturesque, even when bare of leaves. The poinciana is the flower of Puerto Rico.

Bright green leaves up to two feet long are comprised of many tiny, feathery leaflets. The lacy leaves appear in spring just before (or often with) the bloom, which adds to the conspicuous color.

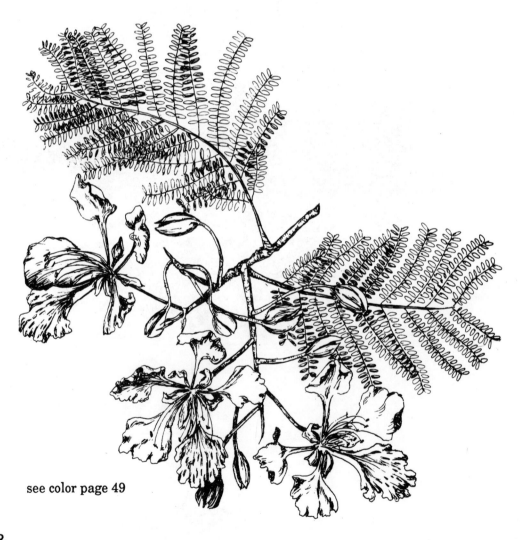

see color page 49

108

Flowers appear in immense clusters, bright scarlet and orange, having five petals – four colorful and one white or pale yellow. The orchid-like blooms are three to four inches across. Following the blooms, the two-foot long heavy, flat seed pods appear and hang on the tree for months, their weight bearing down the branches. In Puerto Rico and some of the other tropical islands the dried pods are used for fuel.

The Poinciana is propagated by seed. It grows rapidly in almost any soil, if it has full sun and a warm climate. In Florida, only the southern half of the state is sufficiently frost-free to ensure the Poinciana's survival. It is, however, notably tolerant of both salt and drought. It has a very aggressive root system. This characteristic, plus its frequent shedding of leaves, flowers, and pods, have lead some people to avoid it, considering it to be a "dirty" tree. However, when these considerations are not of prime importance, and there is room in the landscape for its spreading boughs, the Poinciana is unsurpassed for sheer beauty, color, and brilliance.

Saucer Magnolia

Saucer Magnolia   *Magnolia soulangiana*

This popular, deciduous tree, almost as well known as the Southern Magnolia, *M. grandiflora,* is a hybrid between *M. denudata* (Yulan Magnolia) and *M. liliflora* (Lily Magnolia). The genus is native in Asia, North and Central America. This variety is frequently planted in the southeast U.S. for its early, magnificent bloom — occurring early in the season, and early in the life of the tree. They sometimes bloom when only two or three years old, while *M. grandiflora* may take twenty years.

The large, thick, dull green leaves are obovate, veined, and reach eight inches in length. The six inch wide blossoms are spectacular, appearing as they do in early February before the leaves emerge. Blossoms are deep pink to rosy purple on the outside, with an interior which is white and flushed with pink.

The Saucer Magnolia grows moderately to quickly once it is established, and may be more shrubby than treelike unless properly trained. Like other magnolias, this one prefers rich, deep, fertile, acid soil that holds moisture. It grows best in full sun, but will tolerate partial shade. This variety is hardy and will withstand considerable cold weather. Salt tolerance is fair. The most serious pest is Magnolia scale, a large turtle-shelled scale insect. Magnolia scale may be controlled by spraying with a two percent oil emulsion solution. New trees may be propagated by seed, or by rooting or grafting leafy soft wood cuttings taken in July. Like other magnolias, it dislikes being transplanted.

see color page 62

110

This tree is an excellent flowering specimen for the small garden or large estate. While not as majestic a tree as the Southern Magnolia, its blossoms are showier and more colorful, and will win you many compliments if you decide to choose it for your garden.

Sausage Tree

Sausage Tree   *Kigelia pinnata*

    This tree is an import from tropical Africa, and though it does bloom, it is included as an oddity and not for its flowers, which are more interesting than beautiful or numerous.

    These wide, spreading trees will grow to forty feet tall. The rough, bright green compound leaves have seven to nine oval leaflets which are six or more inches long.

see color page 68

112

The large flower buds hang upright, in chandelier form, from long cord-like stems ranging anywhere from three to twenty feet long. Dark red flowers, four inches in diameter, are tubular, opening to four lobes with the pistil and five stamens rising from the center. Only a few buds open each night and fall in the morning. They have a disagreeable odor which attracts insects. To produce fruit, the flowers must be pollinated early in the day with pollen from another tree. In Africa the flowers are pollinated by bats; in Florida most trees are pollinated by insects.

The fruits are unusual, looking like huge, gray sausages, reaching eighteen inches or more in length and often weighing ten pounds or more. They remain on the stems for many months. They are not edible, but in parts of Africa the natives slice the "sausages", roast them lightly and apply them as poultices.

In frost free areas they are moderately fast growing, preferring sandy loam soil and full sun. Salt tolerance is poor. Propagation is by seeds.

In landscaping it is grown as an interesting specimen, often in parks. The considerable litter from falling flowers and fruit, and the rather unpleasant odor of the blossoms do not endear it as a shade tree on a small lawn.

113

Schefflera

| Umbrella Tree | Octopus Tree | *Schefflera actinophylla* |
| Queensland Umbrella | Brassia | *Brassia actinophylla* |

A native of Queensland, Australia, this popular evergreen is grown extensively in Southern Florida. Since it is hardy to twenty-five degrees, it can be grown in protected areas in much of the state. Its several common names describe its various parts; the shape of the leaf clusters suggests the ribs of an umbrella, while the unusual bloom stalks resemble octopus tentacles, right down to the flower buds which resemble the tentacles' suckers. Like the fabled blind men who encountered an elephant, you can choose the common name according to the part described. However, the name Octopus Tree is applicable only to older trees, as the Schefflera usually doesn't bloom until ten years old.

The tiny, dark red flowers are densely clustered along the slender, radiating branches, two or more feet in length, which protrude from the tree top in early summer. The flowers first emerge as greenish-yellow, turning pink, then brilliant red. They are followed by dark purple, berry-like fruits which harden before the branch falls off.

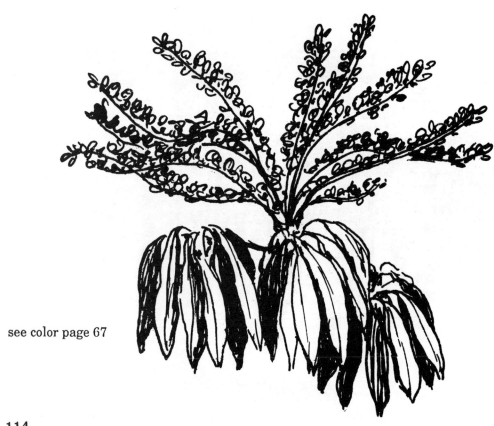

see color page 67

114

While it is often used as a
tubbed specimen in homes or
patios, Schefflera can grow
to thirty feet under ideal
conditions. (Removing the
top stems will keep it bushy.)
The slender upright form,
often with multiple trunks,
grows rapidly in fertile soil.
The leaves are composed of
seven to fifteen slender,
oblong, glossy green,
leathery leaflets. These may
be up to twelve inches long,
and are arranged in rosette
form at the end of a long leaf
stalk, like the ribs of an
umbrella. Schefflera needs
full sun for bloom or dense
growth.

Although we include it as
a flowering tree, it would be
a worthy addition to the
landscape if it never
bloomed. It is attractive for
its foliage alone as a
foundation plant, shade tree,
for framing, screening, or as
a single specimen. Salt
tolerance is fair and it has
few problems. Occasionally
a physiological disorder
causes small lumps to
appear on the leaf, but the
symptoms usually disappear
when new leaves replace the
old.

Shaving Brush Tree

Shaving Brush Tree   *Bombax ellipticum*
                                                        Pachira macrocarpa

Many south Florida gardens are enhanced by this unusual tropical flowering tree. It is a smaller relative of the great Bombax trees. Introduced here as an ornamental oddity, it is native from Mexico to Costa Rica. It is deciduous, producing its showy blossoms on bare branches. It seldom exceeds twenty-five feet in height with a wide spreading crown and brittle branches.

In early spring, before the new leaves appear, dark brown, upright, four-inch flower buds cover the bare branches. They open at night with an explosive sound as the cover splits into five parts and the brownish petals curl back to the stem, disclosing hundreds of pink (or sometimes white) bristle-like stamens, up to nine inches long. Each stamen is tipped with golden yellow pollen. The buds, which yesterday looked like stubby brown cigars, now resemble great pink shaving brushes. (Some people describe them as resembling egret plumes.)

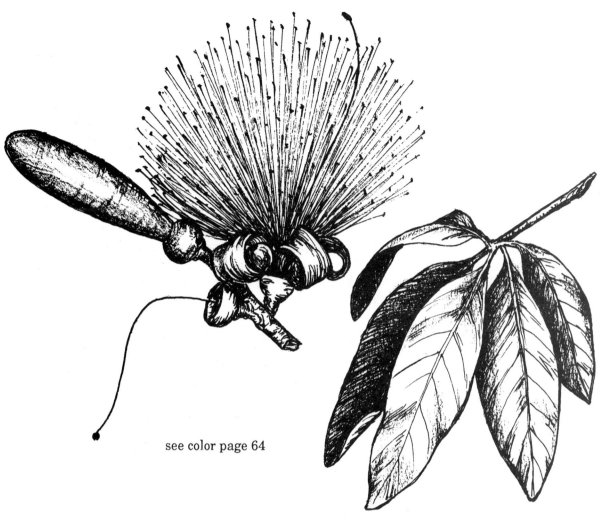

see color page 64

After the flowering period the new leaf growth begins. Leaves are coppery red, and are almost as spectacular as the flowers. The compound leaves consist of five (or occasionally seven) oblong or obovate leaflets, up to eight inches long. As they mature they turn bright green.

This tree grows moderately fast in its preferred environment: a frost free, salt free area, in fertile, sandy, loam soil and full sun. Propagation is by cuttings, air layering, or by seeds if available. Seeds are only rarely produced on the specimens grown in Florida. When they do produce seeds, they are pea-sized and, like others in the *Bombaceae* family, are nestled in "wool" within a large pod.

There is disagreement regarding this tree's Latin name. Though most nurseries will label them "Shaving Brush Tree", they may call it either of several Latin names, depending on the word of which botanist they choose to accept. *Bombax ellipticum* seems the most frequently seen.

A related tree growing in South America is the *Pachira aquatica*, commonly called Water Chestnut or Guiana Chestnut. Its "brushes" are pink or purplish and are followed by foot-long fruits.

117

Silk Oak

Silk Oak   *Grevillea robusta*
Australian Fern Tree

This upright, pyramidal, evergreen tree sometimes grows to a hundred feet or more. It is a native of Queensland, Australia and New South Wales, but has become naturalized and now grows wild in southern Florida. It is not an oak at all, but has acquired that common name because the wood grain resembles oak and is sometimes used for furniture and paneling. The scientific name honors Charles Grenville, a founder of England's Royal Horticultural Society.

The fine, fernlike, grayish-green foliage is two pinnate into lanceolate entire, or lobed segments. The leaves are silvery on the underside and silky in appearance. North of its usual habitat, its delicate evergreen "fern" look has led to its indoor use as a potted plant.

In early spring large, brush-shaped, orange-yellow, odd looking flowers appear in racemes up to four inches long on short branches. Following the bloom is a dry, leathery, one-celled seed pod, which opens along one side only to release the seed.

The Silk Oak is a fast growing tree, easily grown from seed, and is comparatively free of insects. It needs a fertile soil with very thorough drainage. It does not tolerate heavy, wet, or calcareous soil, excessive pruning, or root disturbance.

Although it is considered by some to be a dirty tree, as it drops leaves all year, it has some points in its favor; in our drought prone, sea-surrounded state, the Silk Oak is among the least thirsty trees, and has more salt tolerance than many. It can even stand a few degrees of freezing weather. Such rapid growing, easily maintained trees can provide shade that reduces air conditioning needs (and therefore usage of energy resources), and can help keep the planet habitable through its oxygen for carbon dioxide exchange. Every tree contributes — even those that some may label "dirty" trees! The silk oak can be a valuable parkway tree where water is scarce, and is an interesting specimen in the landscape, for those who like it.

see color page 54

Far less frequently seen than the
G. robusta are two of its Silk Oak
relatives, also from Australia; one
is *G. banksii*, the Red Silk Oak,
which is a ten-foot shrub or
small tree with bright red,
six inch flower spikes. It
blooms occasionally throughout the year, but most often
between January and June.
The other, *G. hilliana*, is the
White Silk Oak, growing to
fifty feet or more. Large
leaves, to a foot long, are
deeply divided and silvery
pubescent beneath. It has
dense clusters of small
white flowers on eight
inch spikes. This
variety is hardy to
twenty-five degrees.

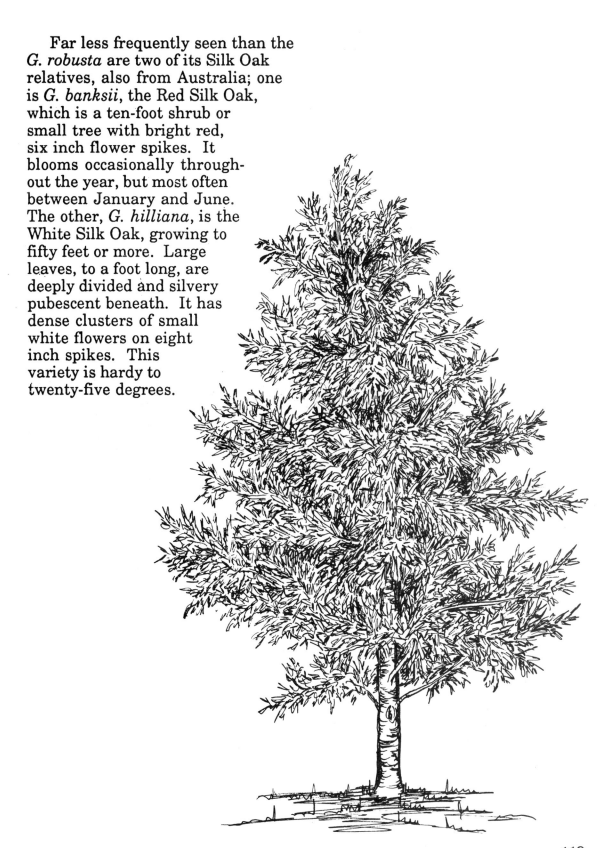

Silver Trumpet

Tree of Gold
Yellow Poui

Tabebuia argentea

The Silver Trumpet tree is semi-deciduous with well-above-the-ground branches growing at awkward angles and covered with light gray, rough textured bark. It is small enough for most gardens, can withstand temperatures as low as most of Florida ever suffers, requires less water than many other trees, and is strikingly beautiful when it bursts into bloom in late winter or early spring.

Among the hundred and fifty known species of *Tabebuia* are some giants of the tropical forests of South America, where their extremely strong, heavy wood is used for lumber. Of the several varieties that have been introduced in Florida, the *T. argentea* is the most common. *Argentea* means silver, a more apt description of the gray-green leaves and silver gray bark than the "trumpets", which are better described as gold — brilliant, glowing gold when seen in the bright sun of a winter day.

The leaves, made up of five to seven oblong leaflets, to six inches long, are light green with silvery scale on both sides. On older trees they are sometimes compound, made up of opposite pairs of leaflets.

The blooming period is irregular, but usually occurs in spring (January to May) just before the flush of new leaf growth. The showy flowers are trumpet-like with five large crepe lobes, bright yellow, growing over two inches long on terminal panicles.

In rich, sandy loam soil, in sun or part shade, the Silver Trumpet is a fairly fast grower. Though some species are quite tolerant of salt, *T. argentea* is not generally recommended as a beach tree.

This is an outstanding flowering tree when used in landscaping as a specimen, a background subject, or as a street tree.

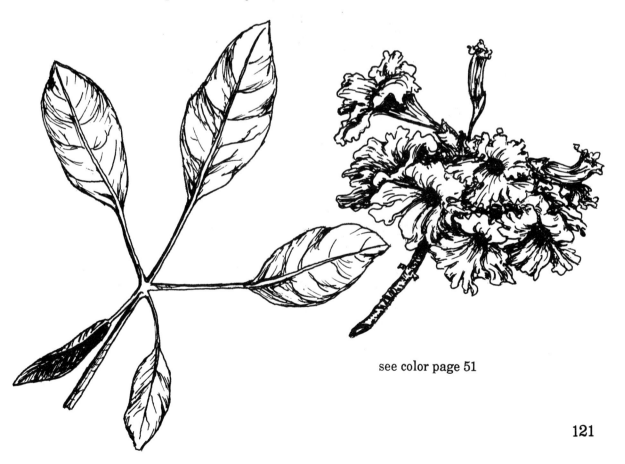

see color page 51

121

Southern Magnolia

Southern Magnolia   *Magnolia grandiflora*

Famous throughout the South, this handsome, stately, evergreen tree reaches eighty feet or more in height and is native to the southeastern United States. The name Magnolia commemorates Pierre Magnol, professor of Botany and director of the Botanic Gardens at Montpelier during the seventeenth and eighteenth centuries. The straight trunk and dense spreading branches of the *M. grandiflora* form a conical pyramid. It is very desirable as an ornamental and shade tree, and is widely used in the South.

Grouped near the branch ends are alternate, thick, leathery, obovate leaves to eight inches long. They are glossy dark green above, fuzzy and rust-colored below, with a prominent midrib.

During spring and summer large, fragrant flowers appear at the ends of short branches. The creamy-white blossoms reach eight inches across, have six to twelve waxy petals, and are very conspicuous among the dark green foliage.

see color page 70

122

The fruit of *M. grandiflora* is brown and cone-like, and has an oval shape. Fruit may reach three inches in length and is protected by sharp spines. The hard, kidney-shaped, brown seeds are covered by a pulpy red skin. When ripe, they are released from the fruit and hang by a silky thread for a few days before falling to the ground.

Southern Magnolias prefer rich, fertile, acid soil, and will grow in full sun or partial shade. Although they may be propagated by seeds or cuttings, a grafted or layered tree is preferable since it will bloom while still small. Trees started from seed may take ten years or more to produce flowers. Established trees are difficult to transplant because their roots are easily damaged. *M. grandiflora* is salt and drought tolerant, and easy to care for.

The Southern Magnolia makes an excellent park, street or shade tree. With its spreading crown, *M. grandiflora* requires a lot of growing space and should be planted at least 40 feet away from other trees or buildings. However, other smaller species, such as *M. acumenata* (greenish-yellow flowers, reddish fruit) and *M. stellata* (small white flowers) may be grown which are suitable as specimen or patio trees. These varieties have the added advantage of bearing flowers when only three to five years old. Many other species exist with flowers of varying sizes ranging from white to yellow, greenish-yellow, red, and purplish red.

Sweet Acacia

Sweet Acacia   *Acacia farnesiana*

Though often found on lists of "native" Florida trees, the Sweet Acacia appears to have come from Mexico and South America; in any case it now grows profusely in the wild in Monroe and Dade counties and to a lesser extent over much of the southern half of the state. It is a smaller member of the six hundred or more species of Acacia trees that have been known and used by man at least since biblical days when it was called Shittah. The name Acacia is derived from a Greek word meaning thorny, an apt name for *Acacia farnesiana*. Two inch spines grow along the branches of this graceful little tree. It grows to a height of only twenty feet, with a drooping habit; the bark is reddish brown.

Leaves are light green, alternate, two pinnate with leaflets to one-fourth inch long. The spines grow from the base of the leaves. It flowers almost continuously, but more profusely in spring, with bright yellow to gold "powder puffs", one and a half inches across, either singly or in clusters. Typical of the Acacia, the fragrance is intermittent, being strong at some times, nil at others. Following the bloom are seed pods, three or more inches long, dark brown when mature and filled with seven to twenty small, shiny, brown seeds. Propagation is by seed.

Sweet Acacia is not as fast growing as many of the flowering trees, but it will grow in poor, sandy soil if given full sun and frost free winters. It is relatively insect free, has good salt tolerance, and meets the criteria of the South Florida Water Management District for use in xeriscaping – that is, it's not a thirsty tree.

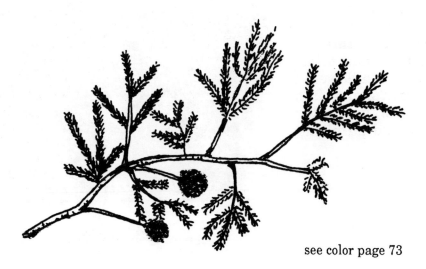

see color page 73

In landscaping, the dainty fernlike leaves and its diminutive size make Sweet Acacia useful as a shade tree in the small garden or patio. A hedge of Sweet Acacias could very effectively deter intruders!

Not all Acacias thrive here, as many require cool nights. Another that does grow well in southern Florida is *A. macracantha*. It is similar in appearance, with golden ball-like flowers, and is armed with paired spines of varying sizes.

Tamarind

Opium Tree

Pithecellobium dulce

Manila Tamarind

This attractive tropical tree is native in Mexico, tropical America, the Philippines, and East India. The name is derived from *pithecos* (ape) and *lobos* (earlobe) so the native name is Monkey's Ear.

The tree attains a height of fifty feet with a spreading canopy. On mature trees, the branches tend to droop, but on small trees stand upright. The gray bark is smooth, the twigs shiny.

Leaves are two pinnate with small, light green leaflets (to two inches), giving the tree a feathery appearance. They fall each year just before the new foliage appears.

In spring tiny, frothy, white, fragrant flowers are borne in dense, round clusters. These are followed by fruit pods, reddish colored, about a half inch wide by seven inches long, and twisted and curled like a ram's horn. When ripe, they split into two parts, revealing the small, black, edible seeds which are thought to resemble opium – hence the common name.

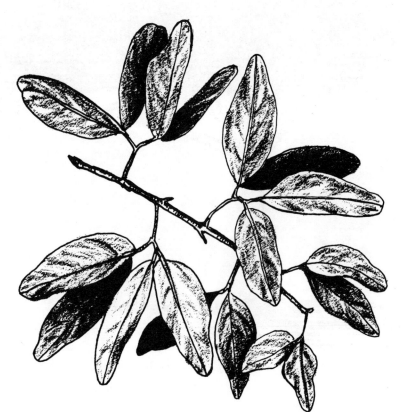

see color page 59

126

The Tamarind is a fast growing tree even in dry, sandy soil. In regions with fertile, moist soil, it responds with vigorous growth. It requires a frost free area and prefers full sun. No pests or diseases attack it, but it does not tolerate salt well; salt spray burns the leaves. It is also rather susceptible to storm damage, as the branches are brittle and break in high winds. Propagation is by seeds. In landscaping, it is used as a shade tree, and was once popular as a street tree.

P. junghuhnianum is a native tree of Java which is sometimes grown in southern Florida. It has orange-yellow flowers in clustered, brush-like heads.

Woman's Tongue

Mother-in-Law's Tongue   Lebbec Tree   *Albizzia lebbek*
Woman's Tongue   Siris Tree
East Indian Walnut

This tropical Asiatic tree grows to fifty feet or more in height, with spreading, brittle branches that form an irregular crown. It gained its "East Indian Walnut" name because its close-grained heartwood is dark brown and very hard – suggesting to some a similarity to the wood of the walnut tree. Some other common names were suggested (perhaps by a man?) by the incessant rattle of the dry seed pods. Light tan, twisted, thick, and a foot long, the dried pods can be quite noisy in the wind. The tree is bare of leaves for several weeks in winter, making the twisted pods even more conspicuous. Early spring brings lacy, compound leaves, to ten inches long. These have rounded, yellowish-green leaflets, about one and a half inches in length, which are arranged in opposite pairs on the stem. Fragrant, plume-like flowers also appear in the spring, in great profusion. They are greenish-yellow and appear in heads or fluffy tufts.

This is one of our most rapid growing trees; it has an extensive root system, which makes it resistant to strong winds. It is hardy enough to withstand winter as far north as Tampa or Orlando. It will do well in almost any well-drained soil, and is recommended for its good drought tolerance. On the other side of the coin, its salt tolerance is only fair, making it a better selection for inland areas than coastal ones. Some people, consider this a "dirty" tree because it sheds either leaves, flowers or pods almost year round. Other people consider this a plus, since the dried pods make excellent mulch when combined with manure, kitchen scraps or other organic materials and allowed to mature for three or four months.

see color page 65

128

This tree is often used in landscaping as a parkway or shade tree. It is easily propagated by seeds, but the seeds must be placed in hot water and allowed to soak for forty-eight hours before planting. The Woman's Tongue tree may also be propagated by cuttings.

Other varieties are *A. julibrissin*, the well known Mimosa that is hardy throughout the southeastern United States. Its light to deep pink flowers are produced during the summer. *A. Kalkora*, from India, has flowers that are yellowish-white with pink stamens and has six-inch pods on long stalks.

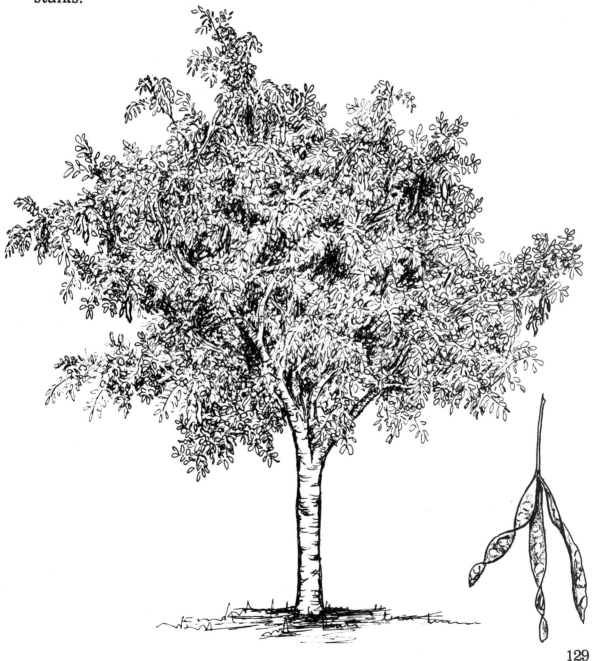

Yellow Elder

Yellow Bell
Yellow Elder
Yellow Tecoma

Stenolobium stans
Tecoma stans

This small tree is a Florida native. It is also native across the Gulf Coast to Texas, and in Mexico, South America, and the Caribbean. It is the official flower of the U.S. Virgin Islands and the Bahamas. The name *Stenolobium* is derived from *stenos*, meaning narrow, and *lobos*, meaning pod; narrow, eight-inch pods bearing thin, winged seeds appear after the bloom. (Some botanists have given it the alternate name of *Tecoma stans*.)

A densely foliaged evergreen tree, Yellow Elder attains a maximum height of about twenty feet. The many bright yellow-green leaves are compound, with from five to ten narrow, sharp-pointed, toothed leaflets up to four inches long.

see color page 76

The showy yellow flowers are borne in great profusion, with as many as sixty growing in one panicle. Each bell-shaped flower is two inches long, and has an orange-striped throat and five rounded lobes.

It has several qualities that recommend it for Florida gardens. It flowers in the fall when few other trees are in bloom. Its fragrant blossoms, lasting up to five weeks, attract hummingbirds and bees. It can withstand light frost, and can be planted near the beach, since it has good salt tolerance. It can be propagated by seeds, cuttings or layering. It is a rapid grower in any reasonably good soil and full sun. It appears to have only two slight disadvantages, both of which can be overcome. It has a tendency to become straggly when not pruned properly, and it may be subject to leaf mites.

Tecoma goudichaudii, from Columbia, is often mistaken for Yellow Elder. It is a shrub or small tree with yellow clustered flowers blooming several times a year.

Yellow Oleander

Yellow Oleander
Lucky Nut
Be Still Tree

Thevetia nerifolia
Thevetia peruviana

This small, spreading, evergreen tree is actually not related to the Oleander. The leaves resemble those of *Nerium oleander*, accounting for the botanical name *nerifolia*. Others have called it *Thevetia peruviana*; the name *Thevetia* is in honor of a French monk, Andre Thevet, who found it on his travels to South America. It has other common names. Be Still Tree may be someone's description of the dense, glistening, narrow (six inches by one-fourth inch), grayish-green leaves, which give the tree a weeping effect. Following the flowers, which appear periodically throughout the year, it produces a one-inch, hard, black, angled fruit. This gave rise to the name Lucky Nut Tree, which may be a misnomer since the fruit, like all other parts of the tree, is highly poisonous. The bright yellow, three-inch long, trumpet shaped flowers grow in terminal cymes, and are delightfully fragrant.

see color page 77

Yellow Oleander grows moderately fast in rich, sandy soil and full sun. It will withstand a few degrees of frost, if it is protected by hilling sand or peat around its base. This tree is not for beach areas, since it has no salt tolerance. It is easily propagated by cuttings or seed.

In landscaping, the dense foliage makes Yellow Oleander excellent for a specimen tree, background planting, or for a hedge which may be clipped to shape.

133

Yellow Poinciana

Yellow Poinciana
Copper Pod

Peltophorum inerme
Peltophorum pterocarpum

Although its common name indicates otherwise, *Peltophorum* is not a Poinciana, just a distant cousin. Native in Ceylon, Malaya, and northern Australia, this tropical, ornamental, umbrella-shaped tree will grow to forty feet or more. The feathery foliage and flowers do resemble the Royal Poinciana, except in color. Considered evergreen in warmer areas, it sometimes sheds most of its leaves in mid-Florida.

The dense, dark green foliage is composed of compound leaves, made up of eight or more pairs of opposite pinnae; each of these have ten to twenty pairs of opposite, small, rounded leaflets. This gives the tree a feathery effect.

The golden yellow flowers appear from May to August in large, upright panicles above the foliage. The many small flower buds are round, and covered with bronze, velvety down which also covers new growth and the midribs of leaves. Opened flowers are fragrant and have five crepy, bright yellow petals that seem to catch and hold the light, and have orange-tipped stamens. The unopened bronze buds and stems are also attractive. Flowers are followed by reddish brown seed pods. They are thin and flat, hold three or four seeds each, and may be up to three and one-half inches long. They remain on the tree for quite a long time, and are sometimes seen along with the flowers.

see color page 66

This fast growing tree needs well drained, sandy loam soil in a frost free area. It prefers full sun and only minimal water; its salt tolerance is fair. It may be propagated by seeds or by cuttings.

Peltophorum is useful in many landscape settings as a specimen shade tree. It is easy to grow and maintain, and its golden yellow flower panicles above the dense green foliage make it spectacular during the summer. Its blossoms retain their golden glow when carried indoors, and are long-lasting in flower arrangements. Their bright color makes them particularly attractive to bees.

P. dubium is a large tree from Brazil with very similar flowers.

Yellow Silk Cotton

Yellow Silk Cotton
Shellseed Tree
Buttercup Tree

Cochlospermum vitifolium

This slender, deciduous, ornamental tree is native in Mexico and in Central and South America. The Yellow Silk Cotton name is appropriate because the shell-shaped seeds (which contribute another common name) are imbedded in a fibrous material rather like that of the Red Silk Cotton or Bombax, to which it is distantly related. It is easy to see how Buttercup Tree became another descriptive name when the golden flowers appear. From January to April, when the tree is quite bare of leaves, bright yellow, cup-shaped flowers, three to four inches across, form in great masses of showy blossoms. After the flowers fade, the fruit capsule forms. It is egg shaped, three inches long, and covered with a soft down.

In early summer the large bright green leaves appear. Arranged alternately on the stem, the five lobed leaves are shaped somewhat like a grape leaf and may be a foot across.

Propagated by seeds or cuttings, this tree is easily cultivated and fairly fast growing in sandy loam soil, in a frost free area and full sun. It can tolerate considerable drought, but is only moderately tolerant of salt. It is used mainly as a specimen tree in the garden.

A double-flowered form of *C. vitifolium* has been developed in Puerto Rico, but it sets no seeds and can be propagated only by cuttings. *C. religiosum*, native to India, is much like *C. vitifolium* and blooms even more prolifically. The bark exudes an amber colored gum which is used in medicine.

see color page 71

Growing Flowering Trees

Soils of South Florida are varied and generally speaking are just a medium to hold the plant up. The deep, sandy soils have very little to offer in plant nutrition and do not have the ability to hold moisture.

Marl soils, which are used almost exclusively for field nursery grown stock, will retain moisture and make a good type of soil for baling and burlapping plants. With proper fertilization and water control, good quality plants are grown.

Muck, which is usually found in lower glades areas, does not have the ability to hold moisture and decomposes rapidly due to bacterial action. Considered a fertile soil, it contains only about two percent organic nitrogen. Many nurseries use a mixture of muck and sand as a planting medium, usually about sixty percent muck and forty percent sand.

Another type of soil is calcareous (lime) rock. The ability of trees to grow in this type of rock is demonstrated in the Redland section of South Florida, where you can see avocado and lime groves at their best.

Plants watered with chlorinated water may develop chlorosis, indicating the lack of an element, usually iron. It is extremely helpful to have your soil analyzed by the Department of Agriculture to determine which elements are needed. The plant may then be treated with a nutritional spray or soil additive, to correct the deficiency.

Deciduous trees should be transplanted when they are bare of leaves. Evergreens will thrive if transplanted at the beginning of Florida's rainy season, around the first of June. If transplanting takes place in the fall or winter, there is a chance a freeze will kill the plant before it has a chance to become established.

Proper pruning is essential in producing most specimen trees. Thinning interior branches admits air and light. This is beneficial to grass or other plants grown under the tree, as well; it is usually lack of light, rather than the tree's taking out nutrients, that precludes the growing of grass or flowers beneath. Begin pruning at the top and proceed downward, cutting flush with the larger branch. Prune to remove dead wood, as it harbors fungi and burrowing insects. If a tree wound is more than an inch and a half across, an asphalt paste or tree paint should be applied. Small trees should be pruned prior to September, so that the flush of new growth can mature before cold weather.

The cold tolerance of plants varies with different genera and conditions. Generally, where "frost free environment" is indicated, the inference is that this particular tree would suffer drastic or permanent damage from exposure to temperatures below 30°F for more than a short period. In some cases, the tree could recover from root stock. A healthy tree should sustain

138

light frost with leaf damage, but without being killed. To forestall damage during a cold spell, trees should be well watered; this is especially true of small trees. If a plant is covered, a frame should be used so that the protective covering is held away from the plant. Spraying with an oil emulsion as a protection is not recommended; it appears to make a tree even more susceptible to cold.

When planting a tree, prepare the hole with at least nine inches on either side of the rootball. Loosen the soil at the bottom of the hole to about a nine inch depth also, to provide room for the roots to grow. Fill the hole with good, black topsoil, cow manure or organic fertilizer, and sand. Set the tree no deeper than it was originally growing, and leave a depression around the tree to aid in watering. When filling in the hole, water well and press the soil down firmly to eliminate air pockets. A mulch of straw, peat moss, sawdust or wood chips around the base of your tree will help hold moisture in the soil during dry seasons. Prune the lower branches and stake the tree until it is strong enough to grow upright and withstand wind.

Fertilizer contains nitrogen, phosphoric acid, and water soluble potash, among other things. The three numbers commonly seen on a fertilizer bag ("6-6-6", for example), indicate the percentage of each of these ingredients, respectively. The remaining percentage (82% in this case) is composed of filler material (such as sand) and miscellaneous nutrients, including elements and organic materials. As a general rule, apply 9-6-6 or 6-6-6 fertilizer about three times a year to each tree, in narrow holes punched twelve to eighteen inches deep, beneath the spread of the limbs. Fertilizer will be more effective if the ground is damp when it is applied and the tree is well watered afterwards. Young trees require more water than older ones. For newly planted trees, water every other day the first week, then twice a week until established. When planting new trees, use a light feeding of 5-10-5 or bone meal. Healthy, well-maintained and well-fed trees are less susceptible to cold and insect damage.

Removal of trees is illegal in many parts of Florida. Permission to cut a tree must be obtained, usually from the local county or city government. In some instances, exceptions are made for designated species. An example is the Melaleuca (Punk Tree), which has become a menace to the Everglades because its prolific spread has tended to replace native species. For this reason, some areas also have ordinances against planting Punk and Brazilian Pepper trees.

Glossary

Acute	Ending in a sharp point.
Anther	The enlarged, pollen bearing tip of a stamen.
Alternate	Leaves placed on a stem, one after the other.
Bipinnate	Pinnate leaflets growing opposite each other on a main stem.
Bract	A modified leaf, differing from the vegetative leaves, usually at the base of a flower.
Calcareous	Having a high content of lime.
Compound	Two or more similar parts in one organ.
Cyme	A flattened flower cluster.
Deciduous	Losing all leaves once each year.
Entire	Having a margin which is not toothed or divided.
Funnelform	Tubular shape of a flower.
Lanceolate	Lance shaped, tapering toward the tip.
Loam	Soil composed of a mixture of clay, sand and organic material.
Lobe	Projection of a leaf; may be round or pointed.
Obovate	Oval, with broader end away from the stem.
Ovate	Egg-shaped with broader end nearest the stem.
Opposite	Paired leaves growing from a common point on the stem.
Panicle	A loose, open, irregularly branched flower cluster.
Pinnate	Featherlike; having simple leaflets on both sides of a common stem.
Palmate	Having lobes, leaflets or veins radiating from a common point; hand shaped.
Pistil	The female organ of a flower.
Raceme	Multiple flower-bearing stalks arising from a main stem.
Serrate	Saw-toothed.
Spine	A sharp, woody outgrowth from a stem.
Stamen	The male organ of a flower.
Strap-shaped	Long and narrow.
Tomentose	Soft and fuzzy; velvety.

140

Index

Other Great Outdoors books for your gardening bookshelf...

Dictionary of Trees (of Florida) Fred Walden	$ 3.95	Landscaping Your Florida Home Maxine Fortune	$ 3.95
Florida Gardening Pasco Roberts	3.95	Handbook of Florida Palms Beth McGeachy	2.95
You Can Grow Tropical Fruit Trees Robert Mohlenbrock	3.95	Handbook of Florida Flowers Lucille Proctor	2.95
You Can Grow Roses in Florida Linus Olson	5.95	Palms and Flowers of Florida Francis Wyly Hall	2.95

Order your copies today from your local dealer. If your
bookseller does not stock these books, send your check to:

GREAT OUTDOORS PUBLISHING COMPANY
4747 – 28th Street North,
St. Petersburg, FL 33714

Please include postage/handling: $1.50 for orders up to $10;
$2 for orders over $10. (In Florida, please add 6% sales tax)